Stephen Kanitz has the habit of writing books that become prophetic. Ten years ago his How to Predict Bankruptcies was a useful tool for businessmen facing the long recession of the 80's.

Veja
**Brazil's most widely
read newsweekly**

*Stephen's recent book is required reading.
It is currently my reference book on Brazil.*

Villas Boas Corrêa
**Political Journalist
and TV Commentator**

MAKRON
Books

BRAZIL

The Emerging Economic Boom

1995-2005

MAKRON
Books

BRAZIL

The Emerging Economic Boom

1995-2005

Stephen Kanitz

MAKRON *Books* do Brasil Editora Ltda.
Editora McGraw-Hill Ltda.
São Paulo
Rua Tabapuã, 1105, Itaim-Bibi
CEP 04533-905
(011) 829-8604 e (011) 820-8528

Rio de Janeiro • Lisboa • Bogotá • Buenos Aires • Guatemala • Madrid • México • New York • Panamá • San Juan • Santiago

Auckland • Hamburg • Kuala Lumpur • London • Milan • Montreal • New Delhi • Paris • Singapore • Sydney • Tokyo • Toronto

Brazil – The Emerging Economic Boom 1995-2005

EDITOR: MILTON MIRA DE ASSUMPÇÃO FILHO

Production Supervisor: Joana Figueiredo
Cover: Layout: Douglas Lucas
Photo: Raul Jr. – Revista *Exame*

Composed by: JAG

McGraw-Hill ISBN 0-07-034084-6

Dados Internacionais de Catalogação na Publicação (CIP)
(Câmara Brasileira do Livro, SP, Brasil)

Kanitz, Stephen Charles, 1946–

    Brazil – The Emerging Economic Boom 1995-2005 / Stephen Charles Kanitz. – São Paulo : Makron *Books*, 1995.

1. Brasil – Condições econômicas 2. Brasil – Política econômica I. Título.

94-2387   CDD-338.9

Índices para catálogo sistemático:

1. Desenvolvimento e crescimento econômico 338.9

To William O. Thweatt, one of the first Brazilianists and one of the best.

MAKRON
Books

CONTENTS

Introduction	. . . .	**XIII**
Chapter 1	**The Growth Surge of the Seventies**	1
	The miracle of cheap financing	1
	Productivity enhanced by high-tech equipment	1
	Industrial expansion assured by a captive market	1
Chapter 2	**What Went Wrong in 1981**	**11**
	The foreign debt crisis	11
	The oil crisis	11
	Foreign banks cut off US$15 billion-a-year pipeline	11
	Without financing, growth comes to a standstill	11
Chapter 3	**The Legacy of the Eighties**	**21**
	U.S. inflation erodes foreign debt	21
	Brazil's tarnished image abroad	21
	The end of the oil crisis	21
	Surge in international reserves	21
	Companies with low debt levels	21

Chapter 4   **Moving into Gear for a New Growth Cycle** **57**

The Exame 500 resume growth 57

Slow privatization is no obstacle 57

Stock exchange boom 57

The wealthy hinterland 57

The success of franchising 57

Popular products, the new avenue for industry 57

A new entrepreneurial mindset 57

Conclusion   **Growth Related Problems** **109**

MAKRON
Books

INTRODUCTION

Good news is no news, goes a saying in journalism. So if newspapers are your source of information on Brazil, you are badly misinformed. There are a lot of positive things going on in Brazil, and the basic theme of this book is that the positives are finally getting the better hand over the negatives, which obviously still exist.

The argument is not that all Brazil's problems are over, but that from now on they are going to be growth-related problems instead of being inflation-related problems.

Businessmen will go on never having a dull moment, but this time around they will be working on problems they can actually solve, rather than reacting to situations thrown at them by dozens of anti-inflation plans.

Brazil will again become a very exciting place in which to do business. Although a resumption of growth is good news, it will be accompanied by fierce competition to be honest, something not all Brazilian businessmen are used to.

The end of inflation is a necessary but not sufficient condition for a country to start growing again. There are dozens of countries with no inflation but no growth either. Something more is needed. Behind all the bad news that has emanated from Brazil over the last 13 years, a lot of positive things have happened but have not hit the headlines.

What would your views on marriage be if you only read the opinions of divorcees on the subject? Among the main sources for economic journalists in Brazil are former finance ministers and former government economists. They have all recently failed to curb inflation, and many were fired. In fact, they have failed, so they tend not to have a positive outlook about the economy, just as a divorcee tends not to have a positive view of marriage.

In the course of a typical week, Brazil's leading business magazine, *Exame*, interviews many ex-ministers but also many a successful businessman. The result is that *Exame* has a much more positive outlook on the national economy than the average daily newspaper.

The point is that the news in print is more negatively biased than the facts warrant. This affects investment decisions not only by foreign investors, but also by local businessmen who are not immune to the bias even though they live in Brazil.

This book sets out to illustrate the following propositions: (1) many of Brazil's alleged problems exist but have been exaggerated; (2) many of Brazil's problems, like the oil crisis, were not self-inflicted but came from abroad; (3) many of Brazil's problems have solved themselves without any active intervention; (4) many problems have been actively tackled and solved by businessmen and government; (5) many problems have not yet been solved, but a resumption of growth will work wonders for them, providing at least partial solutions; (6) not surprisingly,[1] the end of double digit inflation has increased the free time available to decision makers by some 30%, and they can make good use of it to solve other problems than inflation.

Analysis of a country's economy is usually based on factors such as the balance of foreign trade, changes in gross national product (GNP), and interest rates charged by financial institutions, among other macroeconomic variables. Thus it is common to classify a nation's economic performance by looking only at the big numbers.

In this book, however, I focus not on the big numbers but at data resulting from an analysis of thousands of small businesses, top 500 corporations, and 50,000-odd franchises in operation nationwide. These are the relevant figures in a modern economy.

To understand present-day economies, one must analyze a country from the bottom up, not from the top down. One no longer starts with the finance minister and

---

1   Why "ex" – casaram de novo ?

his economic policies. What changes a country are its thousands of businessmen, executives, mom-and-pop stores, franchisors and franchisees. This book may lack the elegance of a treatise on economics, but that is precisely because it deals with so many variables and characteristics at the same time.

Brazil has undergone profound changes in the last ten years but economic statistics do not reflect them clearly. Owing to these changes, the nation has embarked on a new development cycle, which began timidly in 1992, has been consolidated in 1994, and will probably roll on until the year 2005. This will be a new economic miracle, similar to that of the seventies, the most prosperous period in Brazilian history.

We will grow more slowly if we have a federal government that is not capable of moving with the times and using the new management concepts. We will grow faster if our future governments can act as catalysts of growth, instead of insisting on their role as growth generators. Catalysts get the best results with the least effort.

The world has changed. The success or failure of a nation, from an economic standpoint, is no longer determined by grand macroeconomic programs. It is the minor details, the stuff of day-to-day business for small firms and big corporations alike, that have recently come under closer scrutiny. Moreover, they have been mapped out in a great many books on business management, the current fad in the publishing market. Details such as a new entrepreneur's vocation, creativity and determination have changed the profile of Brazilian business and, little by little, have brought to an end an era when the national economy was completely dominated by the big corporations.

This book focuses on Brazil from the standpoint of productive organization, as if the country were a large company. This leads to striking insights, such as, for example, the discovery that Brazil is not a lazy giant buried under the weight of its debts, as IMF economists have insisted on saying for over ten years. We owe very little in relation to our net worth. Brazil's debt-to-equity ratio is less than 4%; in other words, we owe less than 4% of our equity in foreign debt. The problem is that most economists do not reason as if countries were companies, and never even calculate a nation's debt-to-equity ratio.

World Bank economists calculate debt-to-GNP ratios, whereby certain countries end up owing 100% of their GNP, making investors panic and rush to close their savings accounts in American banks with excessive exposure. Debts are repaid not out of annual GNP, but over the contractual term of the debt. If Brazil's debt is divided by projected GNP for the next 30 years, which is the negotiated term for settlement, repayments of principal will consume less than 0.5% of Brazil's GNP per year.

As a matter of fact, this is similar to the situation faced by Brazilian companies, which surprisingly (or perhaps not) have the lowest debt-to-equity ratios in the world.

This book is based on a presentation I have given to more than 100 CEOs, CFOs and Latin American VPs in their yearly round trips to Brazil and Latin America.

Contrary to popular belief, Brazil is not a Boeing 747 flying blind and in need of a competent pilot in the Ministry of Finance. If the finance minister makes a mistake, as finance ministers often do, Brazil flies on nonetheless. This book deals with all the small airplanes that crisscross the skies of the country, instead of finance ministers and economic plans. It is about the real Brazil.

I should like to thank my editor and friend Rosvita Saueressig, who lent clear consistent shape to these ideas.

Stephen Kanitz
Faculdade de Economia, Administração e Contabilidade
Universidade de São Paulo
Caixa Postal 11948 – São Paulo – Brazil
Fax: +55-11-842-5724
Tel: +55-11-843-6783

MAKRON
Books

Chapter 1

THE GROWTH SURGE OF THE SEVENTIES

- *The miracle of cheap financing*

- *Productivity enhanced by high-tech equipment*

- *Industrial expansion assured by a captive market*

The big growth surge in most of the rich countries took place in the mid-1800s, at a time when mechanisms for raising capital, such as Eurodollars, were non-existent. The capital that financed development was generated at great cost from internal savings. Workers were submitted to long hours under wretched conditions, receiving low wages in exchange for the value added.

The capitalist system justified this process of internal accumulation as necessary for reinvestment in new machinery and infrastructure, but it was harshly criticized by Marxist thinkers, who accused capital of exploiting labor. England and the United States, among others, adopted this model during their industrialization process.

In Brazil, new mechanisms such as Resolution 63 and Resolution 4131 opened the door to international savings in the sixties. It is important to stress that there is an immense difference between foreign capital and foreign savings, although most Brazilian intellectuals do not realize this. Foreign capital is the money belonging to multinational companies, which like any investor expect returns of 15%-20% per year on their investment. In Brazil, U.S. investors demand a return of 14% per year or better owing to the inherent risks of doing business in this country.

It is easier to grow by using foreign savings than by generating one's own.

Starting in 1964-65, capital became available directly through bank loans funded by savings deposits in London and New York, which paid interest at 3% per year, after discounting inflation. One of the major mistakes of most debt plans was disregard of the funding angle of the question. Most economists simply forgot that foreign banks were merely debt intermediaries, and that from an economic point of view the lenders were the investors at large. Would any of those investors agree to receive 25% in exports, or debt-for-equity swaps, along with other variations on the same theme, as so many people proposed? Not likely.

For the first time in its history, Brazil had access to very cheap money, with no strings attached, other than loan covenants. State-owned firms and private enterprise invested these funds at the same rates of return, between 20% and 25% per year; the difference between the 3% paid and the 25% earned remained in Brazil. Basically, we grew by substituting financial surplus value for Marxist surplus value. To resort to left-wing terminology for a moment, instead of exploiting its own labor force Brazil ended up exploiting *old ladies* in London, small investors, and a few Arab sheiks who were content with 3% interest per year.

Loans with relatively simple covenants made it easy for companies to grow. When an overseas subsidiary of a multinational transfers capital from corporate headquarters, it also imports management and external audits, an advertising agency and its favorite courier, besides restrictions and limitations such as regular mandatory consultations with head office in the home country. A foreign loan, on the other hand, merely requires payment of interest every six months and a few covenants.

We then embarked on a period of fabulous growth. To a large degree, public opinion mistakenly views any process of indebtedness as negative, overlooking the fact that low-interest debt is the best thing that can happen to a country. What is inadvisable is amassing large debts at sky-high interest, such as 25% per year, as was the case in 1992-1993 with local loans.

One of the most significant indicators of the cycle of prosperity in the seventies was labor productivity, which grew steadily in the period. It stagnated conspicuously in the eighties, which Brazilians call 'the lost decade' (Figure 1).

The best way to increase an employee's productivity is to supply him with more advanced, and therefore more expensive, equipment. There is a visible connection between the capital invested in labor and the productivity of that labor. On average, a Brazilian worker generates revenue of US$98,000 per year while a U.S. employee generates US$250,000 (Figure 2).

In line with a productivity rate almost three times greater, almost three times as much is invested per employee in the U.S. (US$265,000) as in Brazil (US$97,000) (Figure 3). These averages include machinery and equipment, warehouses, and inventory, among other items.

The higher productivity of U.S. employees is directly proportional to the higher rate of capital spending. A closer examination of the figures above shows that Brazilian employees are quite as competent as their U.S. counterparts, since proportionately speaking they produce nearly the same amount. What is lacking is modern machinery to improve overall productivity and enable rates of pay to rise threefold or fourfold, thereby affording incomes on a par with those prevailing in the rich countries.

Figure 1   Labor Productivity
(1971 = 100)

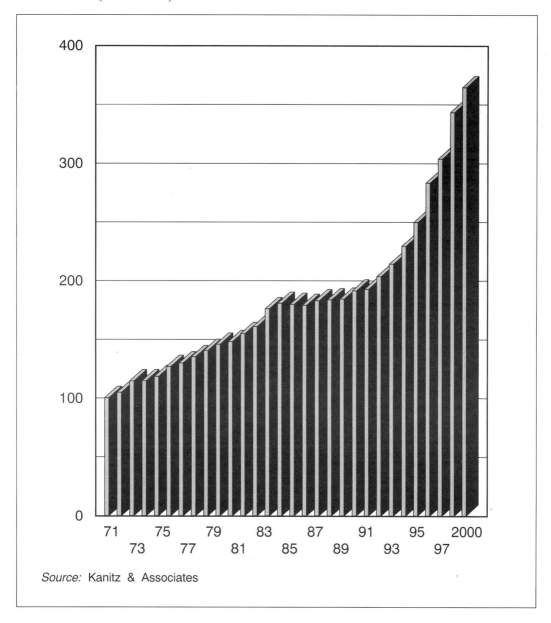

Source: Kanitz & Associates

Labor productivity doubled during the seventies, stagnated during the eighties and will double again by the year 2005.

**Figure 2   Annual revenue generated per employee
(In US dollars)**

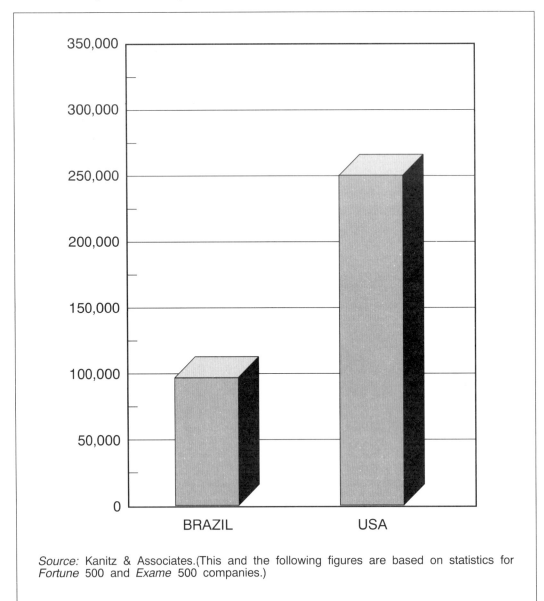

Source: Kanitz & Associates.(This and the following figures are based on statistics for *Fortune* 500 and *Exame* 500 companies.)

(This and the following figures are based on statistics for *Fortune* 500 and *Exame* 500 companies.)

Figure 3   **Investment per employee.**
(In US dollars)

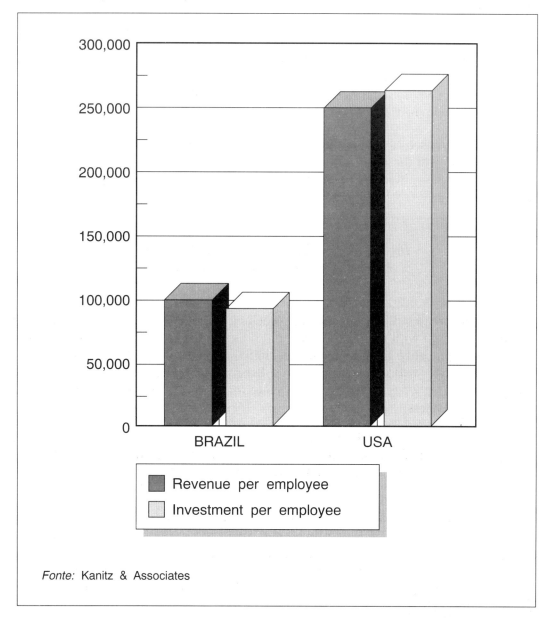

Fonte: Kanitz & Associates

Figures like these are impressive. If we want to generate first-world jobs as former President Fernando Collor liked to promise so insistently we need to invest on average US$290,000 for every job created. Considering that 1.5 million people enter the job market each year, we would need to invest US$435 billion annually.

These, however, are first-world figures. The parameter for the top 500 Brazilian companies is a cost of US$98,000 for each new job, in terms of equipment, facilities and inventory requiring an annual investment of US$147 billion. That is still a very high figure to be financed entirely by domestic savings.

Not all new jobs in the Brazilian economy will follow the standards of the top 500 firms. Many of these 1.5 million jobs will be created by the informal economy, or small firms, where investment is much lower from US$20,000 to US$48,000 per employee.

Buying a job will be the trend for the future.
It is already happening in franchising.

This trend will place a heavier burden on parents. It will no longer be enough to provide a child with a college education to assure his or her professional success. Parents will probably have to obtain the initial capital of US$98,000 so that their offspring can get work. "Buying a job" will be a key future trend. In the Brazilian franchising sector, it has become commonplace for parents to buy their children a small franchise or business.

With the inflow of money from abroad in the seventies, Brazil invested steadily in workers. Because of these factors, from 1936 to 1976 we grew faster than Japan. Brazil lost its place to Japan only because it stagnated during the 'lost decade' of the eighties.

Another aspect worth considering is Brazil's extensive industrial base, built up by the import substitution policy implemented in the seventies. Prohibitively high import tariffs and protectionist policies spurred the economy to start producing all kinds of goods for a virtually captive market. Unlike the Japanese, who specialized in a few areas such as electronics and automobiles, Brazil's industrial sector comprises no fewer than 32 separate branches.

This is a paradoxical situation: on the one hand, it contradicts the precepts of modern economics that recommend a focus on a few sectors, while on the other hand the broad industrial base can leverage economic growth.

The drawback inherent in such a widely diversified industrial base resides in a concentrated business structure with only two or three companies or competitors in each sector, resulting in sectoral oligopolies. In Japan, 12 automobile manufacturers exert cut-throat sometimes predatory competition in the struggle for better and cheaper cars.

Vigorous competition generates far greater business dynamism than is found in Brazil, where a given branch of industry may comprise only two manufacturers who go to the extreme of splitting the market along geographical lines one dominating the market in the Northeast, the other in the South. This peaceful co-existence is healthy neither for the consumer nor for businesses in the long run, since companies that face no competition do not renew themselves as often as necessary.

Trade liberalization, with a resulting increase in imports, will go a long way toward making Brazilian firms more aggressive. Indeed, some great comebacks have already occurred in 1993-1994, and will continue 1995 on.

WHAT WENT WRONG IN 1981

- *The foreign debt crisis*

- *The oil crisis*

- *Foreign banks cut off US$15 billion-a-year pipeline*

- *Without financing, growth comes to a standstill*

Growth for another one hundred years. This would have been Brazil's prognosis based on cheap foreign financing and the profitability it generated. Somewhere along the line, interest rates would have slowly increased and rates of return would have slowly decreased, but that would have taken decades.

Unfortunately, in mid-1981 every single American bank cut off credit lines to Brazil, Mexico, Argentina, Chile, the Philippines, and 60 other countries. Brazil's growth cycle shuddered to a standstill. Most experts, among them IMF economists, attribute this event to problems such as an imbalanced economy, excessive debt, monumental overspending on infrastructure projects, and government incompetence. But this raises a simple question: how can it be that these countries, all recipients of loans in the international market, were doing the wrong thing at the same time? What did Brazil have in common with the Philippines, a country with a totally different economic and political system?

To repay the loans taken out to finance the Itaipu hydroelectric plant, for example, the plant had first to be brought on stream. The electricity it generated was designed to make production possible for companies whose exports would bring in foreign currency to repay the debt incurred by building the plant. Every banker knew that Itaipu by itself would not generate foreign currency. Not only did the end of new loans prevent completion with foreign loans,of the plant, but Brazil was left without the capital to build the industries that would have produced the exports.

If we look at Brazil as a business corporation, we will find that its US$180 billion in foreign debt corresponds to less than 4% of the country's equity.

Another interesting point is the fact that not a single banker was willing to go on lending money to those countries. In a free enterprise society like the U.S., there is always someone who is willing to go against the grain. When the market falls, there is always some maverick who buys stock. Why weren't there any nonconformist bankers, not a single one?

Economists in general do not analyze a country's performance like that of a company. If we look at Brazil as if it were a business corporation, we can see that at that time for a net worth of US$3 trillion, there was US$180 billion in foreign debt less than 4% of the country's equity. The average Brazilian company usually operates with a

50% debt-to-equity ratio. For U.S. companies, the ratio is vastly higher: for every US$100 of equity there is an average of US$280 of debt. A debt-to-equity ratio of 4% is ridiculously low.

Brazil's problem was not its very low debt-to-equity ratio, but lack of liquidity: international reserves had fallen to zero after the prime rate began rising in the early eighties. An analogy would be millionaire Scrooge McDuck shopping without a single coin in his pocket. He would still be rich, but would be unable to pay for a slice of bread owing to lack of liquidity, not excessive indebtedness. Any banker would lend Scrooge McDuck money under such circumstances, although he would of course require collateral to secure new loans.

Another issue on which public opinion has not been properly informed is how Brazil could go broke when paying only 4.5% real interest per year. During that period (1981-82), real interest rates were a little higher than the historical average of 3%, owing to a surge in inflation in the U.S. They were still low interest rates, however much lower than the average rate of return obtained by Brazilian companies. In 1990 domestic interest rates in Brazil soared to 22% per year, and even then few companies filed for bankruptcy or protection from creditors. Why should Brazil go bankrupt at a time when interest rates were 4.5% per year on the international market?

Actually, it was not the high level of indebtedness or the disorganization of our economy that brought growth to a stop in Brazil. It was a minor error by the U.S. government in regulating American banks. U.S. banks are not allowed to lend more than ten times their capital. This regulation has been copied by central banks all over the world, including Brazil's. The restriction is supposed to be a guarantee of financial prudence that will prevent a private-sector bank from lending above its capacity and jeopardizing the entire financial system.

U.S. banks' balance sheets are not adjusted for inflation and their equity therefore suffers erosion.

U.S. legislation does not allow inflation accounting in the form required under Brazilian rules. No foreign executive in Brazil would accept a salary in Brazilian currency without an inflation adjustment clause, usually pegging it to the dollar.

As a consequence of the extremely low annual inflation rates in the U.S., the American financial system failed to see the need to provide for inflation in its contracts and legislation. However, over long periods of time this minor mistake has had damaging effects on the US banking system. Just imagine what has happened to the initial capital of the Bank of Boston, founded in 1776, with no inflation adjustment for over 200 years. The book value of its initial capital has been totally eroded by 200 years of inflation. So have its retained earnings for 1882, 1902, etc. So has Bank of Boston's lending capacity.

Because the Comptroller of the Currency does not allow U.S. banks to adjust book values, institutions have consistently lost lending capacity. This is one of the hidden causes of the decline in the U.S. economy. The U.S. economy has lost its lending ability because of a flaw in its banking regulation.

U.S. banks have tried to circumvent these problems by operating off-balance sheet lending, derivatives, and a number of other fancy products that do not involve loans. Even off-balance sheet financing has become regulated. Because of a simple banking regulation, U.S. banks are playing the risky derivatives game, despite its limited economic value. The problem is that they cannot earn money the old-fashioned way – by lending.

The meteoric rise of Mike Milken and the Junk Bond movement was due not so much to his genius as to the fact that he had no competition. Banks could not compete because their lending ability had been destroyed by two years of very high inflation, in 1980 and 1981, and an average rate of 4% a year thereafter.

U.S. banks then lost their supremacy to the Japanese, who not only had a low inflation rate at the time, but had better bank regulations.

Brazilian banking legislation is more modern; it allows banks to lend up to 12 times their equity, adjusted yearly for Brazilian inflation. Someone might argue that for accounting reasons American banks are more profitable than Brazilian banks. Since neither equity nor assets are adjusted for inflation, the American bank's profit is therefore overestimated. But even if we accept this line of argument, it would not make any difference if a U.S. bank reinvested all the overestimated accounting profit. The effect would be neutral because the two mistakes would cancel each other out.

The unfortunate fact is that the U.S. Internal Revenue Service does not see it that way and demands 50% of the bank's 'inflationary' profits; the shareholders, usually conservative people, demand another 50% of the balance, or so-called retained earnings, as dividends. In practice, U.S. banks cannot compensate for the inflation effect and what often seems to be an accounting profit is actually a loss.

The inflation effect in the U.S., historically in the 4% range, used to be compensated for by banks' high profitability, around 12% per year. This ensured that equity increased faster than inflation.

This equilibrium came to an end in 1981 when inflation got out of hand, surging to 10%, and then to 12% the following year. The equity of financial institutions was eroded, and they started to show a loss. Companies started defaulting, and provision for loan losses depressed profits. Profits became negative, thus reducing equity even further. The effects of U.S. inflation could no longer be offset by a high rate of return. All banks without exception exceeded their lending limits, and all at once halted their loans to Brazil, Mexico, Chile, the Philippines, and other countries.

This situation lasted until 1983, when U.S. banks started finding loopholes in these credit restrictions, in the form of derivatives operations that are not recorded in the accounting books and are known as off-balance financing. Banks started operating as guarantors, enabling loans to be made by other organizations such as pension funds, which at the time were looking for profitable investment to cover their growing actuarial needs for payment of benefits.

These loopholes, which stem from the inability of U.S. banks to lend money through traditional operations, were later to become the flourishing derivatives market. Nearly ten years later the market has practically forgotten how to make a 'plain vanilla' loan.

The abrupt halt to bank loans in 1981 caught Brazil by surprise, of course, with neither inventory nor the necessary financial structure. The country was scheduled to receive US$15 billion; when this did not materialize, adjustments had to be made.

The consequences affected practically all areas of the economy and caused the postponement of many plans. We ended up having an electric power surplus for nearly 15 years because there was no financing for new firms that could consume the power generated by the Itaipu hydroelectric plant.

During this period, Brazil was perceived as a poorly managed, financially incompetent nation with too heavy a burden of debt, no reserves, and an extremely high credit risk rating. None of this was called for, given the above analysis.

It was at this time that the IMF and the World Bank began arguing that Brazil ought to to implement a structural adjustment, i.e. develop a plan for economic stabilization. What should have been done instead was to make the necessary adjustments to U.S. banking legislation, so as to require banks to record U.S. inflation in their books. That would have benefited both the Brazilian and the American economy.

It is a shame that U.S. banks stopped lending to Brazil, not because its economic framework was in disrepair, not because the level of indebtedness was too high, but because of mistaken U.S. regulations for the banking industry.

The debt crisis profoundly altered the relationship between the international financial system and the so-called emerging economies. In 1986, the governments of the rich countries ratified the Basle agreement, hindering both new loans to the Latin American nations and mortgage lending in the U.S. real estate market, another whopping financial scandal at that time.

The only way for Brazil to regain access to external savings is through foreign pension funds.

Loans started to be weighted according to risk-based criteria. Thus, a loan to Latin America could cost 120% of a bank's equity, whereas a loan to a U.S. corporate client would cost only 100% of the company's equity – the wrong solution to the wrong problem.

The U.S. legislation was not modified but, if anything, made more restrictive after the Basle agreement. Worse still, even though successive Brazilian ministers and Central Bank teams have negotiated on the foreign debt, at no time has the demand been raised for a change in U.S. banking restrictions. That is a shame, because the U.S. banks' very ability to lend is itself at stake. The industry has lost its lending capacity for ever.

The only way for Brazil to regain access to external savings will be by means of foreign pension funds, since these organizations are not regulated by the U.S. Comptroller of the Currency. Pension funds can lend in proportion to their assets, which are hedged against inflation by being mostly invested in short-term markets such as stock exchanges. Nearly 80% of the money that has flowed into Brazil in recent years came from pension funds.

Economists at the IMF only made things worse. Under their influence, Brazil implemented a series of completely mistaken measures. Several stabilization plans were introduced, but all failed. The currency was sharply devalued and pay rates were drastically reduced in order to make exports more competitive. Brazil became a huge exporting machine in order to respond to the banks' problem of deteriorating assets, steadily eroded by U.S. inflation during the eighties.

World commodity prices plummeted, compounding the problem. The currency was artificially undervalued to help exporters, and imports of all kind were kept in check by various means.

Meanwhile, banks started insistently demanding repayment of the debt in order to comply with inflation-eroded lending limits. It is curious that they were unable to realize that this process resulted in the destruction of the U.S. banking system. During the ten years of the Brazilian foreign debt crisis coinciding with the 'lost decade' – financial institutions suffered as much as Brazil in terms of setbacks and losses.

Japanese banks became the biggest in the world, because their equity is adjusted for inflation.

The Japanese financial system eventually overtook America's. With a more effective set of laws, the Japanese banks ended up being the biggest on earth. Japanese legislation allows real-estate gains to be incorporated into stockholders' equity, whether such gains relate to branch premises or other properties. This is fairly similar to, or even better than, what happens in Brazil with inflation accounting and revaluation.

The Japanese shrewdly decided that they could create wealth and enhance lending ability simply by increasing the value of the real estate market. The more their facilities grew in value, the more they could lend; it was like being able to print your own money. They started lending massively to the real estate business. Bankers were responsible for the real estate boom in Japan, because it generated even more lending ability.

The Japanese real estate boom burst in 1989, leaving banks in a similar situation to U.S. financial institutions in 1981. The drop in value of their real estate assets forced them to backpedal and ask Japanese corporate clients to repay their loans. This situation will stabilize only when the inflation curve in Japan meets the descending curve of real estate values. At the point in time when the two curves meet, the Japanese economy will once more be in balance. That may take another decade.

Figure 3B   Japan's ability to lend.

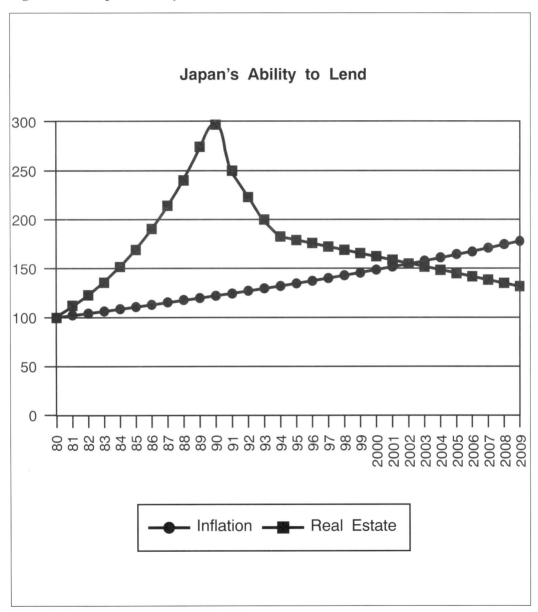

Land values and japanese inflation.

MAKRON
Books

Chapter 3

THE LEGACY OF THE EIGHTIES

- *U.S. inflation erodes foreign debt*

- *Brazil's tarnished image abroad*

- *The end of the oil crisis*

- *Surge in international reserves*

- *Companies with low debt levels*

There was nothing structurally wrong with the Brazilian economy in 1981. In fact we were getting along fine in terms of growth. The big mistake was not understanding the dynamics of bank regulation. But then neither did the U.S. government. More than 13 years have passed, and we reach the first good news in this book.

Over the years, without anyone noticing, and with no headlines, Brazil's foreign debt has slowly been eroded by U.S. inflation.

The same inflation that ate into banks' assets ended up eroding Brazil's foreign debt. To a lay person, Brazil owed US$100 billion in 1982. If you look at the numbers now, through the eyes of the Brazilian Central Bank or the IMF, the debt seems actually to have grown bigger over the years despite every effort made by the IMF and all the adjustments made by the Brazilian economy.

This is the traditional interpretation of the figures published by the Central Bank and the IMF and, I might add, an incorrect one. The correct calculation must take into account accumulated U.S. inflation of nearly 80% in the period 1981-1992, the effect of inflation averaging 4.5% per year, and two years of high inflation at the beginning of the decade. As a result, the US$100 billion Brazil owed in 1982 becomes US$180 billion in current dollars, adjusted by U.S. inflation (Figures 4, 5 and 6).

If we include U.S. inflation during that period, we find that the 1982 value of the foreign debt goes up to US$180 billion. Currently the debt is estimated at only US$130 billion; the difference is due to the effect of U.S. inflation. Since Brazil's foreign debt is not index-linked, the effect of U.S. inflation is an annual erosion of around 4.5%. During this 13-year period, it has diminished to about 60% of its original value.

Considering that Brazil has accumulated US$35 billion in reserves, its net debt drops to US$95 billion, practically 50% of what it was. This same result can be demonstrated in a different manner. In 1982, our net foreign debt corresponded to 56% of GNP; it currently corresponds to only 15%. Add in the fact that it will be paid off over a 30-year period, and you have less than 0.5% of GNP per year. Peanuts.

In 1982, a group of German banks got together to discuss a common strategy on the Brazilian debt 'problem'. The outcome was a plan to reduce the overall debt in various ways to 60% of its original level, a more manageable and digestible amount, and take it from there. With this 60% reduction, loans could be resumed, probably at a more judicious pace than in the seventies, but at least it would be back to business.

Basically the 60% level has been reached, and lending has in fact resumed, through Euronotes and Eurobonds issued by Brazilian companies.

Figure 4   Brazil: Foreign debt.
(In billions of US dollars)

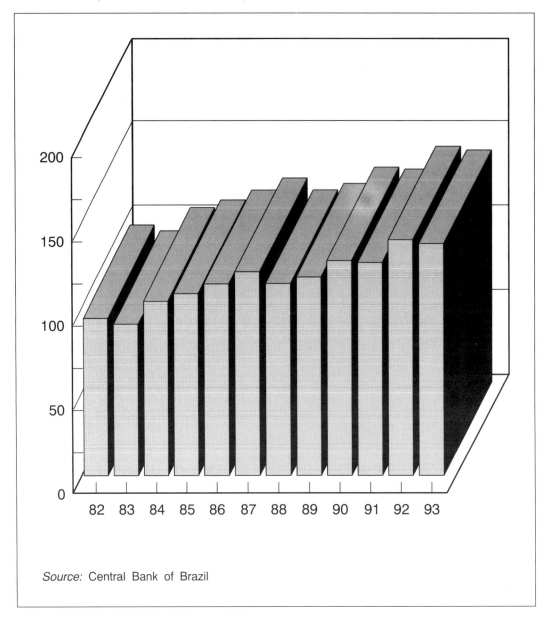

Source: Central Bank of Brazil

Brazil's foreign debt seems to grow when analyzed by its nominal value.

**Figure 5   Brazil: Erosion of foreign debt.
(In billions of 1993 US dollars).**

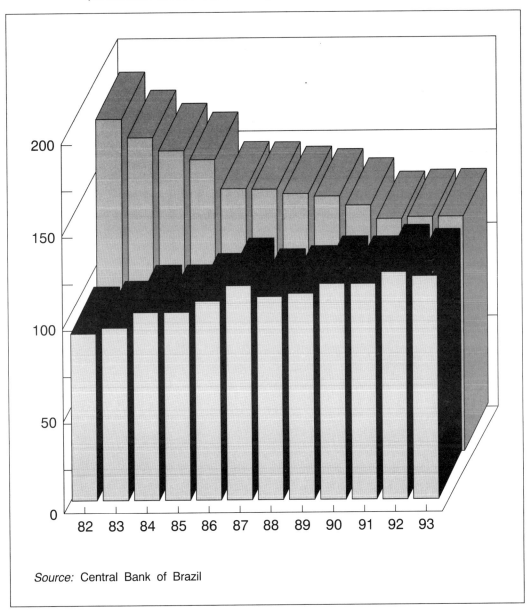

Source: Central Bank of Brazil

Net Brazilian foreign debt is corroded by U.S. inflation and drops 50% in twelve years.

**Figure 6   Brazil: Repayment of principal.
(In billions of 1993 US dollars)**

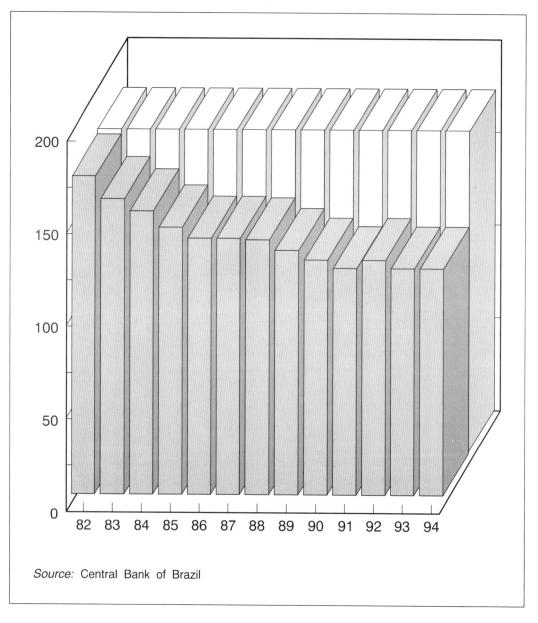

Source: Central Bank of Brazil

The debt was indirectly repaid by payment of interest with built-in U.S. inflation.

Because the lending limits on U.S. banks have yet to be adjusted to American inflation, bank loans will not be the main source of foreign lending to Brazil and Latin America. Funds will be raised through private placements directly to pension funds. Indeed, that is exactly what is happening with the new Brazilian Euronotes.

The conventional wisdom over the past 13 years, even among influential or well-informed citizens, is that Brazil has not repaid one single cent of principal over the years. On the contrary, runs this version, additional debts have even been accumulated, mainly because of interest payments in arrears, thereby compounding the problem.

The conclusion to be drawn from this reasoning is that one of the main factors that brought growth to a halt in 1981 has disappeared. The foreign debt problem is no longer a concern. As any banker knows, a company that cuts its debt volume by half solves its debt problem entirely.

Today Brazil has a marketing problem, not a debt problem.

Brazil is AA investment grade. It has always paid the real interest rate and has now repaid half of its original debt.

I once called on the Central Bank official responsible for publication of data on the foreign debt. I tried to persuade him to take into account the effect of U.S. inflation, which was to reduce the debt's value from one year to the next rather than increasing it as the Central Bank statistics would have us believe.

In reply, the official said this was not a good idea since in the eyes of the international financial community we would be demonstrating Brazil's ability to repay its debt. Bankers would probably demand more and more payments. This conversation took place in 1986, when Brazil was accumulating reserves. Hence the concern to ward off demands for debt payments to be stepped up.

The very idea that we were negotiating with bankers is wrong. Bankers are simply brokers. Brazil was in fact negotiating with grannies in London and John Doe in New York, and with banks' stockholders, who are often simple people with no technical expertise. These people have funds but little time to think about Brazil. All they want is to see Brazil's debt shrink. In fact, international bankers and the Brazilian government had a common enemy: bank stockholders and small investors.

Being trained in finance, U.S. bankers knew about the debt erosion phenomenon but kept quiet, because they knew that the inflation that erodes debts is already built into U.S. interest rates. LIBOR and the prime rate always reflect U.S. inflationary expectations plus a real interest rate. When U.S. inflation reached 14% per year, interest rates went up to 21% per year.

From the semantic point of view the debt was not really eroded by inflation. It was simply repaid, or prepaid, which is financially more correct. Over the years, Brazil has in fact secretly repaid most of its original debt. Not only has all the annual real interest been paid, but US$50 billion in principal indirectly built into interest rates has been repaid.

The logic of a financial system in which borrowers repay only a small percentage of a loan at maturity, because of the effects of inflation, is beyond the comprehension of most Brazilians.

Most credit-rating organizations miss out on this logic completely. A country that reduces its debt by one half, has a trade surplus that is three times the real interest paid, and has always paid the real interest on its debt is definitely investment grade. That is not the picture one gets, however, from Standard & Poor's, Moody's and the EIU Country Risk Service.

Many investors made the same mistake, and took horrendous losses. At one time the average discount on Brazilian debt reached 80% of its face value, a totally unreasonable discount given the fundamentals just analyzed. The debt which investors were selling at an 80% discount was being repaid in real terms every year. Brazil's ability to pay was never in jeopardy from an economic point of view, but owing to faulty nominal analysis, no one realized that a hefty principal prepayment was built into interest rates. The Dart family were right to buy up practically 5% of Brazil's debt.

In 1995, Brazil's average discount should drop to zero. There could even be a premium, depending on the ratio between the coupon rate and current interest rates. Another problem out of the way.

Figure 6A   Country Risk – Mistaken Calculations.

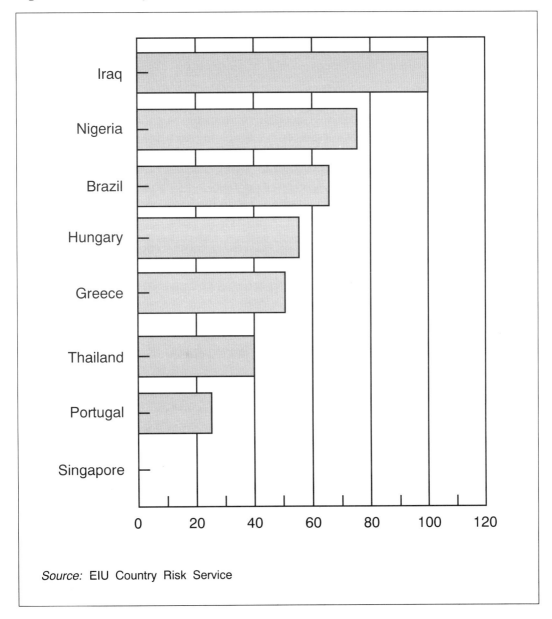

Source: EIU Country Risk Service

Brazil has managed its image poorly.

The world airline industry has suffered badly because of this same accounting mistake. So have Nabisco, Donald Trump, and most leveraged buyouts. When nominal interest rates are charged to income, they erroneously deplete profits. Accountants worldwide are running principal repayments through the profit and loss statement – a gross mistake. Principal repayments should be booked directly as an offset against liabilities. Otherwise profits are understated, investors and creditors panic, and no-one realizes that inflation will increase the value of the assets bought with the debt in question. Unfortunately that will only become obvious ten years down the line, when airlines for example will resell their planes at a much higher price than book value.

International capital markets tend to swing sharply whenever interest rates vary between countries simply because inflation rates have changed. Yet real interest rates remain practically the same. So much for not living in the real world, and making nominal-world mistakes.

At the Congressional hearing into the effects on the U.S. banking system of Brazil's decision to suspend payments on its debt, a New York banker argued that the creditors would 'stop receiving principal'. This was a Freudian slip.

The tragedy is that a company which pays interest punctually, repays half its total debt over the years and has a debt-to-equity ratio as low as 4% is more likely to be rated AA or A than BB, as Brazil is rated by too many people.

Brazil has managed its image poorly.
We have been unable to show the world that we are a good credit risk.

This is the great national tragedy of the lost decade. During this period we were considered bad debtors, poor credit risks, financially disorganized, and so forth. Everything we were not, in other words. The incompetence for which Brazil should be blamed during this period is bad management of its financial image. We failed to show the world that we were honoring our financial debts in real terms. We share this situation with Chile, Argentina, Indonesia, the U.S. and other countries that lacked the skill to show the world their real face. The U.S. Congress is unable to show the American people that the federal deficit is not as big as critics say, simply because it is calculating nominal rather than real interest payments, and real interest is usually half the value of nominal interest.

The second tragedy is that the IMF economists went around the world telling countries to adjust their economies, when the problem was that the U.S. Comptroller of the Currency and U.S. banking laws were out of step with the reality of inflation accounting. It does not make sense to use historical accounting values to set lending limits in an inflationary environment. To this day the IMF does not realize the damage done to 800 million people.

The next reason why Brazil stopped short in 1981 was the second oil shock, which drove up the price of crude nearly threefold from US$12 per barrel to US$33 per barrel. The latter price would be US$55 in today's dollars. Yet 13 years later, a barrel of crude costs between US$14 and US$16, just over a third of the price paid in 1981.

The second oil shock was also eventually eroded by inflation and partially offset by the numerous energy conservation measures adopted worldwide from then on. The price of oil in 1993, US$14 per barrel, was equal to the real price of oil in 1973, two decades ago (Figure 7).

The drop of some three-fourths in the price of oil means more than a reduction in transportation costs and reimbursements of salesmen's fuel expenses. This price drop is equivalent to about 1.2% of GNP in terms of disposable income for the average Brazilian population. The cost of oil is pervasive; it accounts for a large proportion of the price of every product. Thus even those who do not ride cars or buses enjoy an increase in purchasing power. The income now available to the population reaches the incredible sum of about US$80 billion.

Unfortunately, the population is not aware of this increase in purchasing power because the 'Arab tax' as the steep increases in oil prices were dubbed – has been replaced over time by inflation tax and interest rates.

Figure 7   Oil price falls.

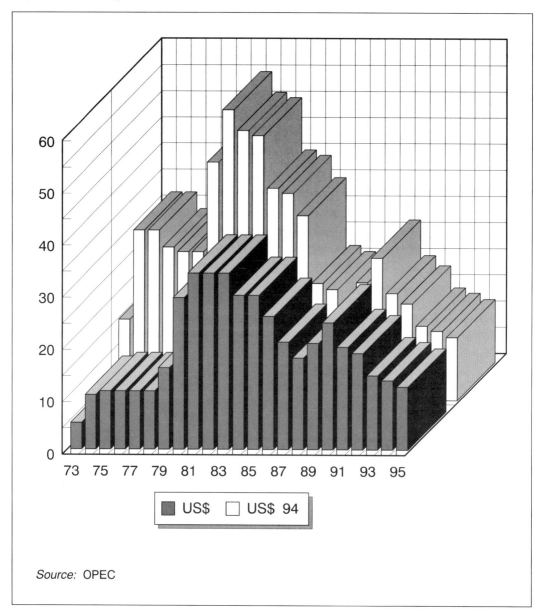

Source: OPEC

The price of oil falls to one fourth of its value in a period of 13 years.

Nothing fosters growth like low interest rates.
Nothing hampers growth like high interest rates.

The third factor that brought Brazil's growth to a halt in 1981 was high LIBOR, which reached 21%. This was actually a fictitious rate, since it reflected high U.S. inflation that year, plus 4.5% real interest. Americans do not use inflation accounting; they add inflation to their interest rates, giving the investor the impression that the yield is actually 21% per year, when it is not. Spend the interest rate year after year, and you will discover that you have been dipping into your capital, and so has Uncle Sam through the tax he collects.

In 1981, banks were in fact paying interest at 4.5% and were repaying principal to investors at a rate of 14%. Brazil was making interest payments on its debt and also repaying 14% of the principal. In 1981, it suspended not interest but these principal repayments, which had not been negotiated.

The reality was that the foreign debt was being repaid in advance owing to U.S. inflation. Years later, international interest rates dropped to the 3% level, bringing Brazil back to the comfortable position it had enjoyed in the seventies, when international savings were available at interest rates that were highly favorable to growth. Nothing fosters growth like low interest rates. Nothing hampers growth like high interest rates (Figure 8).

Another piece of good news is that over the years Brazil was able to accumulate massive reserves of foreign exchange. From zero in 1981, it had built up US$40 billion by the early nineties, equivalent to about 30% of the foreign debt. In fact, this figure is excessive in relation to the size of the economy and the foreign debt. Yet it highlights another curious phenomenon: Brazil's financial credibility is not proportional to the size of its reserves (Figure 9).

Figure 8   International interest rates fall.

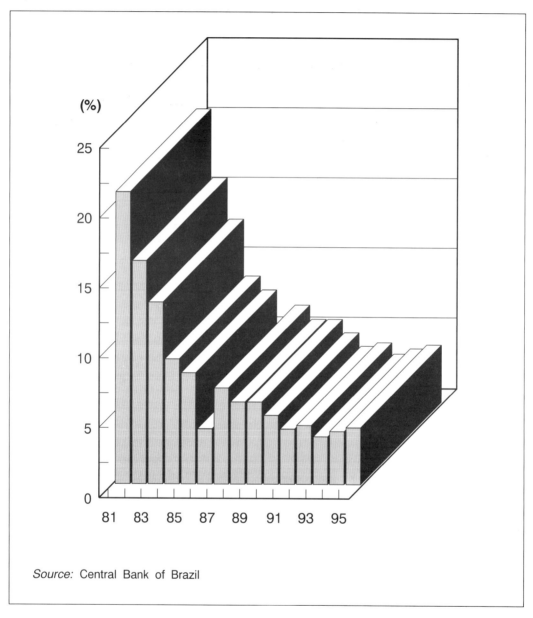

Source: Central Bank of Brazil

International interest rates fall 80% in twelve years.

**Figure 9   Brazil's international reserves resurge.
(In billions of US dollars)**

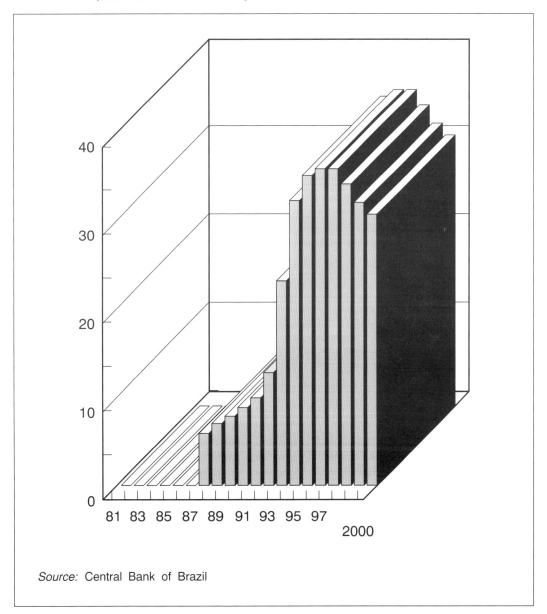

Source: Central Bank of Brazil

Brazil's reserves reach first-world levels.

For many years Brazil needlessly courted the IMF. If someone had to be courted, it should have been the analysts working for Moody's and Standard & Poor's. In the nineties, these organizations have become essential to countries interested in attracting pension fund investments. It is unlikely that commercial banks will ever operate as they did in the past. Banks will operate as co-signers and guarantors for the credit operations Brazil negotiates abroad; they will no longer make direct loans.

Organizations like Moody's and Standard & Poor's will make a prior appraisal of issuers and grade them on a scale from D to AAA. Any country or firm that takes its relationship with these two institutions lightly is bound to pay a very dear price when it seeks foreign financing.

A case could be made that if all the effort expended on keeping the IMF happy had been used to establish good relations with these two credit-rating organizations, Brazil's reputation would have been better served.

Another question that should be analyzed is the discount on Brazil's foreign debt. In 1990, a bond issued by the Brazilian government could be bought abroad for 24% of its face value. Many politicians and economists interpreted this piece of information simplistically, assuming it meant that Brazil owed only 24% of the bond's value, since that was its market value. On the contrary, the huge 76% discount indicated a brutal increase in the interest rate or country risk as it was erroneously perceived. The discount was a reflection of Brazil's poor credit rating as perceived by the international market (Figure 10).

Every country's government should strive to reduce its perceived risk as much as possible. In fact, countries should strive to sell their bonds at a premium. The sweetest dream of any central bank governor should be to see his country's bonds being traded at a 10% premium, i.e. a bond with a face value of 100 being traded at 110. Since the 1990 debacle there has been a steady fall in the discount on Brazil bonds, and as a result Brazil's risk rating has also fallen. That is why we will soon be opening our doors to low interest rates. The sad part is that this discount was applied to Brazil unfairly, since we have never ceased to be a good credit risk.

Figure 10   Discount on foreign debt.

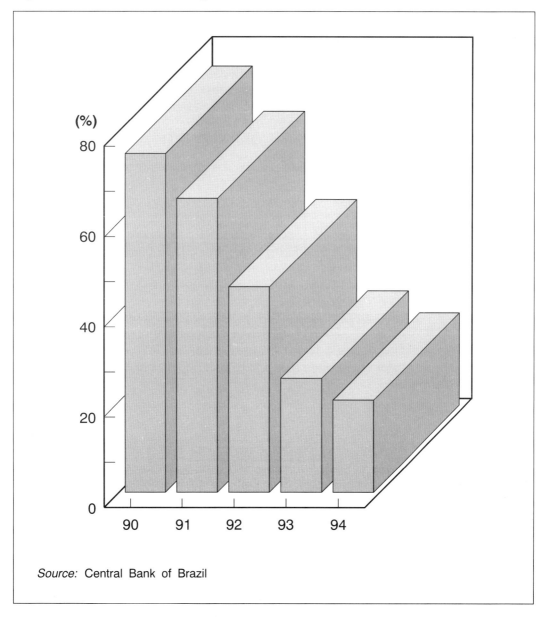

Source: Central Bank of Brazil

Brazil recovered international credibility when the discount rate on its debt bonds dropped.

I have set out to show that Brazil had one of the highest growth rates in the sixties and seventies, and that we know how to grow. In this we are different from Eastern Europe, which lacks a business culture, managers, and the accounting and administrative systems necessary for growth. Brazil has all of these. Our managers may be a little rusty, but they basically know their trade.

We stopped growing in 1981, let me stress once more, not because our economy was a shambles or because of overwhelming structural problems but because of a minor error in the U.S. banking system, which does not adjust bank loans to allow for U.S. inflation. This error was responsible for stopping an international credit flow of about US$15 billion per year during the seventies.

In practical terms, Brazilian companies are the least indebted in the world.

Because of high interest rates during the eighties, Brazilian companies used all the cash generated by operations to liquidate their debts. They did not lose their investment capacity, but used it to retire debt, instead of buying new equipment.

Even though they did not create new jobs or expand, these companies made the best possible investment by ridding themselves of an obligation to pay 20% interest per year. Few companies obtain a return on investment of 20% per year at no risk. Reducing the size of a debt involves no risk, whereas setting up a new plant or investing in production always carries an inherent risk of failure.

Ironically, this process came to an end in 1991 and 1992 because Brazilian companies had no more debts to repay. The alternative was to redirect investments toward their own business again. Of course, some companies chose instead to go after a quick buck in the money market, but not as often as the public thinks. The figures clearly confirm this point. The average Brazilian company invests 10% of its liquid assets in the money market. The remaining 90% is invested in fixed assets, inventory, production, equipment etc. It is not correct to say that the majority of company profits come from the money market.

Contrary to current opinion, Brazilian companies' debt-to-equity ratios are among the lowest in the world. For every dollar of equity, Brazilian companies owe 50 cents. American companies' leverage is much higher; for every dollar of equity they owe US$2.50. One of the secrets of the Japanese miracle is that Japanese businesses have always been highly leveraged, and their economic model depends on a high debt-to-equity ratio: every yen of equity corresponds to 3 yen of debt. Their money is even cheaper, since real interest rates in Japan are around 2% per year, while return on investment averages 12%-14% per year (Figure 11).

Figure 11   Corporate debt-to-equity ratios.

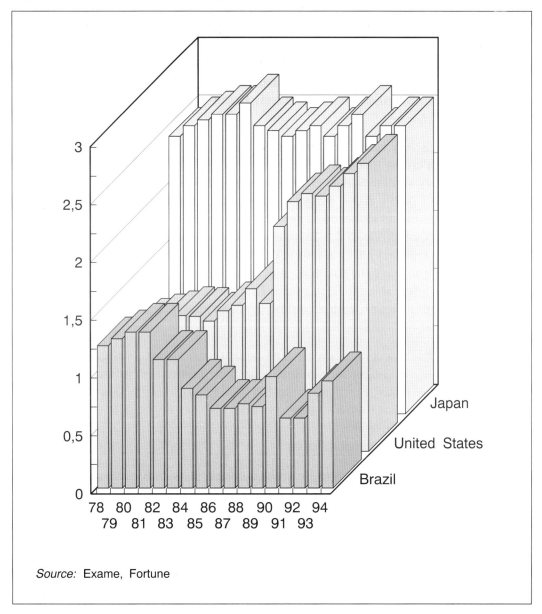

Source: Exame, Fortune

Brazilian companies are among those with the lowest debt burden in the world.

During the lost decade, Brazilian executives avoided debts like the plague. The result is that we now have companies with a strong capital base, ready to support a new acceleration of growth and indebtedness. In spite of heavy losses and recession, Brazilian firms enjoy good enough financial health to lead the country along a new path of rapid growth. The same potential cannot be clearly perceived in Argentina or in Mexico. In fact, few Brazilian firms went bankrupt in 1990, 1991 and 1992, during the worst recession in Brazilian history, precisely because businesses had a strong capital base.

This is a very important factor from the standpoint of economic growth and leads to the conclusion that Brazilian firms are about to embark on a new cycle of indebtedness, very similar to that of the seventies. This new debt cycle, stimulated by the availability of credit at 3% per year in the international market, will spur Brazil toward new investments and production. By the year 2000 the debt-to-equity ratio of Brazilian firms is set to rise to 2.5. In other words, they will have 2.5 reals (the current name of Brazil's currency) of debt for every real of equity the same ratio as U.S. firms. Thus Brazilian firms have the financial structure to accumulate four to five times their current debt at affordable interest rates. This reflects huge growth potential. The resumption of foreign loans, with an inflow of cheap money, should bring about a drop in average interest rates in Brazil.

The top 50 banks worldwide lend only 0.6% of their portfolios to Brazil, a figure totally out of proportion to the country's importance in the international economic scenario. Brazil's GNP accounts for 2.8% of world GNP. This would be a fair ratio to apply to the allocation of funds to Brazil. Thus we ought to be receiving 2.8% of the world's foreign investment and savings, just as we should be receiving 2.8% of the loans granted by international banks.

That would mean another fivefold increase. It is likely to occur as soon as there are signs that Brazil's inflation problems will not rebound.

The risk is that politicians and economists will take a jaundiced attitude to this new surge in debt, seeing it with the same prejudiced eyes as they did in the past. Brazilian public opinion is biased against foreign debt, which it mistakenly considers the main obstacle to economic growth. It fails to take into account the fact that foreign interest rates are much lower than rates on the domestic money market (Figure 12).

Figure 12   The new debt cycle.

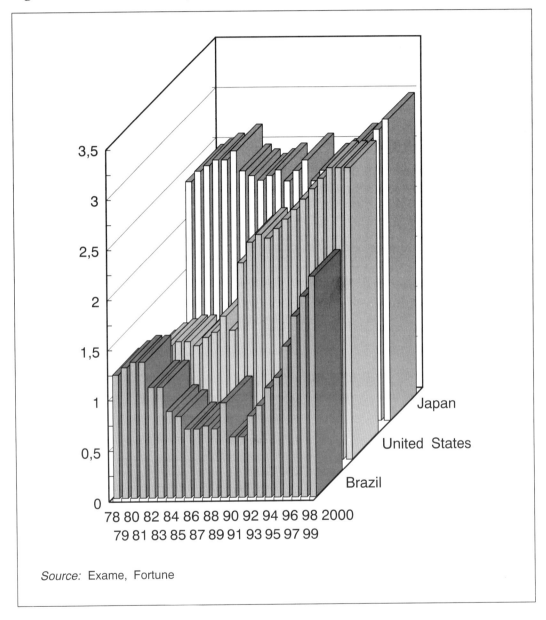

Source: Exame, Fortune

Brazilian companies will embark on a new debt cycle to finance their growth.

For years, debt was seen as the main reason for Brazil's stagnation. Several political campaigns were based on promises by politicians to renegotiate or even suspend payment of the foreign debt. It will not be easy to convince a whole generation that the reason for our economic stagnation was precisely the opposite – a lack of financing or of cheap loans. The risk of misinformation remains, insofar as some Brazilian economists are already worrying about the increase in the level of debt, as if this were a negative event.

International bankers, as we have seen, were not exactly blameless in the episode of the foreign debt 'crisis'. They did not explain to public opinion in Brazil that the real interest rate on their loans was much cheaper than local money market rates. In effect, for Brazilian banks the debt 'crisis' eliminated precisely those competitors (foreign lenders) who offered loans at much lower interest rates. Brazilian bankers, in fact, were quite content to see the debt crisis eliminate foreign competition.

International bankers are more competitive because capital is cheaper and more plentiful in developed countries than in emerging economies. Money is more expensive for Brazilian bankers because capital is scarce.

Politicians and public opinion should be persuaded to come around to the view that no barriers are needed against the inflow of foreign loans to finance Brazil's new growth cycle. What should be demanded from the government is an end to floating-rate loans.

Foreign investors will also show a renewed interest in Brazil, as long as returns are compatible with the international market.

Government budgets do not allow for floating-rate loans because they entail open-ended interest payments.

It is often argued that we need multinationals for the technology they possess, not because of the capital they bring in. However, we will never have access to their technology, even if we pay royalties. Surely a Brazilian entrepreneur with the same capital as a foreign company would create just as many jobs? Bank loans are not tied to the same conditions as capital invested by multinationals. These loans assume at most a detailed contract covering interest rates, due dates and a few safeguards against misuse of funds borrowed.

This is why foreign loans are much more useful than foreign capital.

When inflation comes to an end, which it already has, the world will see Brazil in a different light. For the old lady in London and the investor in New York, living with 40% inflation per month is inconceivable. It reminds them of the chaos of the Weimar Republic. They are unable to grasp the indexation mechanism which enables us to live with galloping inflation without destroying our economy completely.

The Real Plan – the latest anti-inflation plan – is not an economic plan, as most of its predecessors were. It is an accounting plan. Roughly speaking, it entails translating everything into dollars, more or less as U.S. subsidiaries in Brazil do with their accounts every year. The Cavallo Plan in Argentina did the opposite. In Argentina, they do their purchasing in dollars and their accounting in pesos. For a short while only, the Real Plan involved keeping accounts in dollars and making payments in cruzeiros.

Over a two-year period inflation had increased from 25% to 45% a month. Those who understand the mechanics of monthly indexation will know what I mean when I argue that the real inflation rate was actually only 10% a year. Because of indexation, any price increase perpetuates itself for ever. In Brazil, a U.S.-type inflation rate of 5% a year would automatically compound to 79% (1.05^{12}) a year, because we have monthly indexation, while the U.S. has annual indexation.

Inflation in Brazil should be understood as being the sum of two parts: indexation plus additional inflation. So what Americans and Europeans call inflation is in fact add-on inflation in Brazilian terms. Thus the war on inflation in Brazil was effectively won in 1993, because the add-on inflation rate was then running at 10% a year. For readers who are economists, the actual rate is somewhat higher say 30% a year, but by Brazilian standards that is still a victory.

The problem was therefore how to get the self-perpetuating effect of indexation out of the system, especially because it had reached 40% a month. The Real Plan did just that. For readers who are engineers, the Real Plan was a clever way of performing a rotation of the coordinate axis.

Leaving the details aside, there are two points that make the Real Plan different from its many unsuccessful cousins. It was the first plan not to create pent-up inflation during the intermediate stage, ready to explode when the plan reached completion.

Figure 12A   Inflation rate up only slightly in three years.

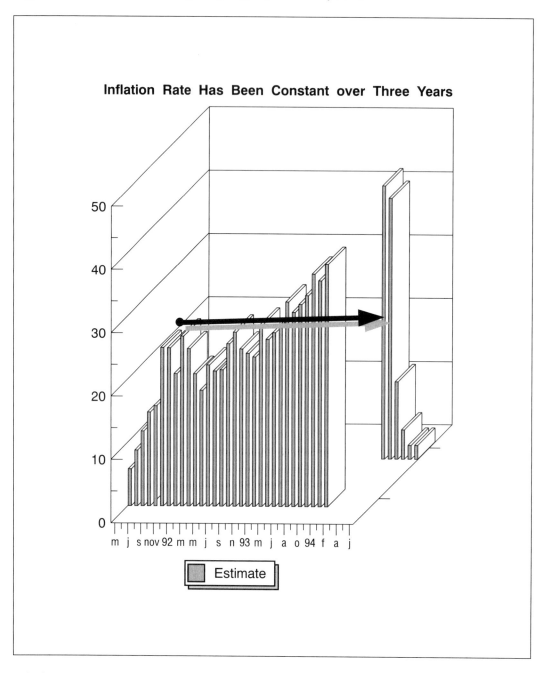

Inflation actually ended in 1992.

Under previous programs that centered on price freezes, suppressed inflation would burst back into life as soon as the price freeze was lifted. In Argentina, there is pent-up inflation of 18%-25% which the government hopes will eventually be absorbed by greater productivity. We will have to wait and see how the Cavallo Plan finishes up, when the exchange rate is finally allowed to float freely.

Every plan has a beginning, a middle and an end. The Real Plan can be said to have ended on July 1st 1994, when the currency was transformed or rotated on its new axis. The truth is that the *Real Plan has already successfully reached completion* and inflation has not rebounded as at did at the end of the last two plans. Two months after the end of the Cruzado Plan inflation was over 14% a month; two months after the Collor Plan it was 24% a month. Three months after the Real Plan, it was less than 2% a month, with no pent-up inflation to worry about.

The Real Plan was also the first not to distort the price system in Brazil, unlike the Cruzado Plan which destroyed it with a price freeze.

These two considerations justify the forecast that inflation will not rebound in the near future   at least not with the explosive viciousness of the past. It was accelerating at 10% per year before the Real Plan, which was a simple accounting plan involving no economic wizardry or changes to the structure of the economy.

Inflation may creep back slowly over the years. But never again will Brazil see inflation at 40% a month   or 30%, or even 20% a month. A 10% rate may appear for some freak reason, but only for a month or two. In an emergency of that kind, given that Brazilian economists have learned the trick, they would at once roll out Real Plan II.

The stage is therefore set for growth-inducing inflation rates of 2%-3% a month, not growth-hampering rates of 40% a month. And growth works wonders by spreading fixed costs and encouraging price reductions without reducing profit margins. Hidden behind past inflation rates are margin losses of 30% in dollar terms in construction, appliances, and other industries.

There is another sense in which the Brazilian plan is quite different from the Argentinian plan, though they may seem similar to the naked eye. If the Cavallo Plan should flounder two months after the exchange rate is allowed to float, we will not need to start worrying about Brazil's future.

Though government officials tend to be perfectionists, the best bet is that inflation will not be licked completely at the first shot. Possibly at some point during 1996, a second stage will be required for fine tuning. If so, a no- traumas plan similar to the Real will eliminate whatever residue there happens to be.

International economic statistics are collected on a calendar-year basis. The low rate of inflation in Brazil during the second half of 1994 was not enough to offset the soaring rates occurring in the first six months. From the statistical standpoint, the 1994 inflation rate will still be high. Only when a low inflation rate is recorded for 12 consecutive months, i.e. in 1995, will the international statistics-gathering organizations detect a drop in Brazil's inflation.

Not until March 1996 will these figures show up in IMF and World Bank reports, and in *Time* articles. Only then will small shareholders in U.S. banks or small investors in London learn about the demise of Brazilian inflation. There will then be a great surge in foreign investment in Brazil, at long last. Comparing an inflation-free Brazil with Argentina, Chile and Venezuela will be too easy, an almost cruel pushover, for Brazil. Only in the case of Mexico will foreign investors have some doubts a toss-up.

Given that in the seventies there was an annual inflow of US$15 billion, it is reasonable to project US$30 billion with the end of inflation in the nineties. Probably there will be much more. This forecast is no exaggeration in the global economy of the new world order. In fact, I would venture to predict that the *annual* inflow between 1995 and 2005 will range from US$36 billion to US$45 billion.

New loans are already being made, in the form of private placements of Euronotes issued by Brazilian firms. Moreover, the coupon rate is lower and will continue to fall to around 7% in 1996, adding another positive aspect to Brazil's economic boom: cheap money.

Figure 12B   Euronote coupon for the average local issuer.

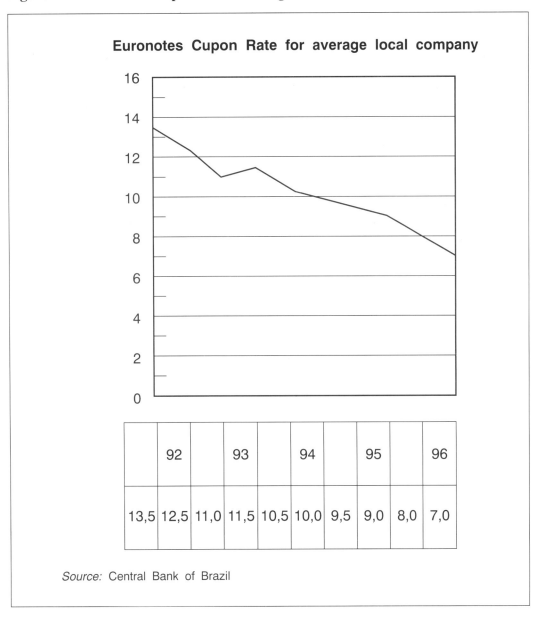

Interest rates will go down.

The volume of international inflows will not be even higher only because the Brazilian economy cannot handle more. It cannot adapt fast enough. It was administratively unprepared to manage the volume of money that came in during the seventies, although technically the economy was in good enough shape to absorb it.

Neither government officials nor public opinion are prepared for the high-growth scenarios discussed in this book. No plans for such optimistic situations have been drawn up, and this might result in lower growth. There might be bottlenecks such as a shortage of products in certain markets. Opening up the economy further will allow imports to overcome these temporary scarcities. Some difficulties remain, however. It will be impossible to import electric power, for instance, and there will certainly be supply shortfalls. Government and business will have to make every effort to conserve energy and invest heavily in the power industry, as the rest of the world has already done.

The growth that began in 1993 was attributed to a temporary spree by consumers. Now there is a feeling that Brazil is really growing again.

Brazilians usually panic at the mere mention of a shortage of electric power, because they know it takes ten years to build a hydroelectric plant. In fact, this is not the only solution. There are other sources of electricity, such as thermoelectric plants, whose basic equipment is a turbine that can be imported in less than six months and brought on stream in 18 months. The power shortfall scenario should not frighten anyone. This obstacle can be overcome, albeit at a potentially higher price than if plans had been made ahead of time.

Brazil overlooked the need for investment in power generation and other areas because the prevailing atmosphere was overly pessimistic. Neither the deterioration of the foreign debt nor the resumption of economic growth was then in sight. The feeling that Brazil is growing again, in a sustainable manner, is now ratified by some experts. The growth recorded in 1993 was initially seen as a 'bubble', the result of a short-lived spree by consumers.

There is so much capital available in the world, I repeat, that there is a shortage of investment opportunities to use up the supply coming from pension funds, insurance companies and intensive savings-generating entities.

U.S. pension funds are in a panic. Actuarially they need a real rate of return on investment of about 6% per year to cover their social security commitments. Many have even greater needs. Since real interest rates in the U.S. are now around 3% per year, pension funds must seek more profitable investments, even if that means taking higher risks. This is a growing trend, reinforced by longer life expectancy in the rich countries (Figures 13 and 14).

Some time around the year 2000, General Motors (and many companies like it) will have more retirees than working employees on its payroll. As a result, the inflow of social security contributions from GM's employees will be lower than its expenses with retirees. The first visible result of this search for more profitable investment is the boom on the São Paulo Stock Exchange in 1994, caused by the massive inflow from foreign pension funds. Even under unfavorable conditions, with a 40% monthly inflation rate, Brazil was still attracting investments in need of high returns. Imagine the inflow with low inflation rates.

There are around 80,000 pension funds worldwide. The largest U.S. pension fund Teachers Insurance Annuity Association (TIAA), with 1.6 million participants has a portfolio worth US$100 billion.

That is why, in spite of Brazil's lack of credibility and the financial marketing mistakes of the past, we will start receiving foreign money once more. It could even be said that these investments are lining up to enter Brazil, since there has never been any institutional advertising by Brazil to show institutional investors where the US$150 billion has been invested. Brazil should have spent about 0.1% of this total on advertising, merely to reassure the dozens of investors who believed in our country. This would have considerably reduced risk rates and spreads. Brazil's biggest private-sector banks, like Bradesco and Nacional, spend proportionately far higher amounts on advertising to attract customers.

Another auspicious element in our economy is the advent of modern manufacturing techniques like just-in-time and *kanban*, which have cut production costs and eliminated the need for factory inventories. Between shifts a huge empty space that used to be occupied by parts inventories is often to be seen inside plants. When companies regroup their machinery, eliminating the empty spaces between them, they discover a whole new plant inside the old one. Very little additional investment will be necessary for companies to grow once more. When the Brazilian economy picks up speed again, the first 18% growth will probably be obtained at low cost, because firms will need to buy the machines required for expansion but not land or warehouses.

**Figure 13   The return of foreign investment.
(In billions of US dollars)**

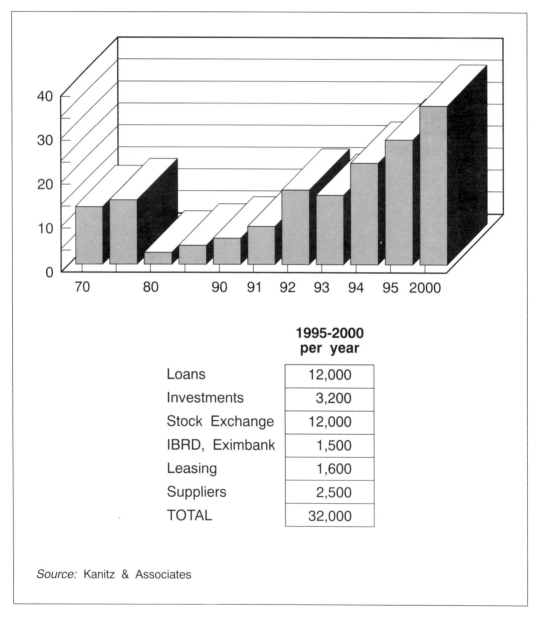

	1995-2000 per year
Loans	12,000
Investments	3,200
Stock Exchange	12,000
IBRD, Eximbank	1,500
Leasing	1,600
Suppliers	2,500
TOTAL	32,000

Source: Kanitz & Associates

The inflow of foreign funds will grow a great deal in the next ten years.

**Figure 14   Pension funds in search of attractive investments.
(In billions of US dollars)**

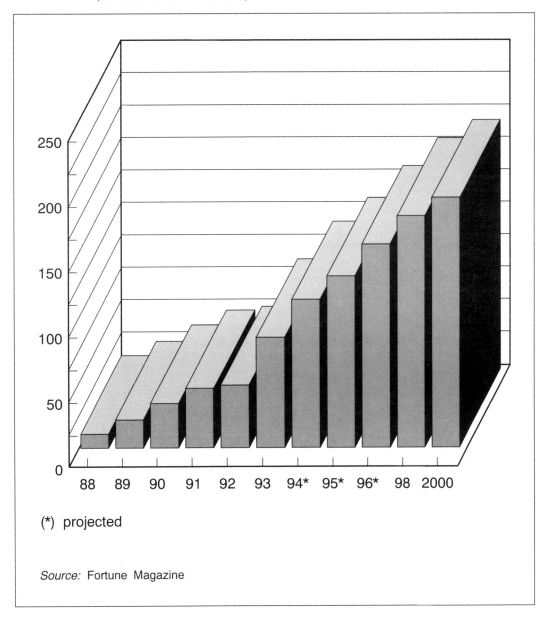

(*) projected

Source: Fortune Magazine

U.S. Pension Funds plan to invest US$180 billion per year abroad.

When the economy starts growing again, profitability will be higher than in the seventies.

The crisis was cruel, but it taught Brazilian firms a great deal. Downsizing has enhanced productivity by eliminating superfluous management levels and rationalizing production processes. Our business culture, essentially family-centered and paternalistic, constituted an obstacle when the time came to fire employees who were no longer productive after 40 years of service but had been kept on for sentimental reasons. The 1990-92 recession was so brutal that it brought this paternalism to an end. Two or three levels have been removed from the hierarchy. All this has resulted in satisfactory gross profit margins well above world averages, in fact.

Gross profit margins (on individual items, as distinct from a firm's average profit margin) have been restored. Take the example of a regular airplane flight. Once breakeven has been reached, each additional passenger means a straight profit, except for the coffee and food served on board. This is sometimes what is called the contribution margin. For Brazilian firms, it is around 30%, well above the international average of 18%-25%.

Our companies will be very profitable in 1995 and 1996, thanks to their high gross margins. Since Brazilian firms traditionally reinvest 80% of their profit, when the economy starts growing again these high profits will be invested in production and development.

Reinvestment of profit was the only source of funds available to Brazilian firms after the loans dried up. The 1986 suspension of foreign debt payments eliminated any remaining chances of obtaining external loans. Local credit lines were unaffordable. National savings were siphoned off by the Brazilian government to finance the public-sector deficit. High domestic interest rates affected stock prices, which began a slow and steady decline, making the stock market unattractive as a form of financing for corporate growth.

That is why, of the four financing alternatives foreign loans, domestic credit, stock market, and reinvestment of earnings only the latter remained as a source of funds. After the disastrous Collor Plan in 1990-1991, when 52% of Brazilian firms took an operating loss, the option of using earnings for investment also vanished. That was the start of the worst recession in the country's history, with three years of total stagnation. During the 1929-33 recession in the U.S., only 30% of all businesses suffered losses.

When Brazilian companies started showing a profit again in 1993, reinvestment of earnings became viable as a financing alternative.

Banks stop being inflation hunters and return to their traditional lending activities.

The stock market reacted in 1993-94 and a second alternative became available: capitalization through equity issuance. The end of inflation brought lower interest rates and greater access to domestic financing. This in turn stimulated consumer credit and encouraged businesses to raise money by discounting trade bills, both of which were typical banking operations during the seventies, before banks became inflation hunters instead of money lenders. Once inflation is perceived to have been brought definitively under control, the stock market will become even more bullish, and foreign loans will return en masse. We will have recovered the four sources of business financing; growth will consolidate and become self-sustaining.

We will also have recovered a country with new prospects. The pace of business as it returns to a predictable and steady flow will give the economy a fresh boost. It will be similar to the euphoric days of the sixties and seventies, except that it will be built on a more solid foundation. The nation is more mature, with decentralized administration. There is a whole generation of managers who have been to business school and are better trained. Equally important, we have learned from our past mistakes.

There is a particularly intriguing novelty in this new growth cycle: profit margins, which have traditionally been high in Brazil, will tend to fall as competitiveness becomes steeper. By 2000, profit margins are likely to have fallen to somewhere between 20% and 25%. However, at the first surge in growth, Brazilian firms will enjoy higher profit margins than their counterparts in Argentina, Venezuela and other neighboring economies.

The good news about the performance of Brazilian firms came in 1993, with most businesses showing a profit again. In the previous three years, average profitability had been negative for the first time in Brazilian history. In 1993, there was an average profit rate of 3.5%, still low compared with the historic average of 14%.

The sales margin, i.e. the ratio of profit to sales, has also climbed to more attractive levels   around 2.5% of sales. This detail is often overlooked when performance is analyzed. It means that for every 100 reals of sales, a firm obtains a profit of 2.5 reals. This is a low rate, but it is in accordance with the worldwide trend of reducing the rate of profit on individual products. Firms have steadily squeezed the profit made per unit sold, but offset this trend by raising production volume, thus boosting profit overall. By keeping prices low and volumes high, they guarantee a high return on the capital invested. In 1993 and 1994, profit margins went up to 3.5%. They will probably not rise further to 4%, the average rate in the seventies and eighties, because competition is now sharper (Figure 15).

Figure 15   Projected profit margin (profit as % of sales).

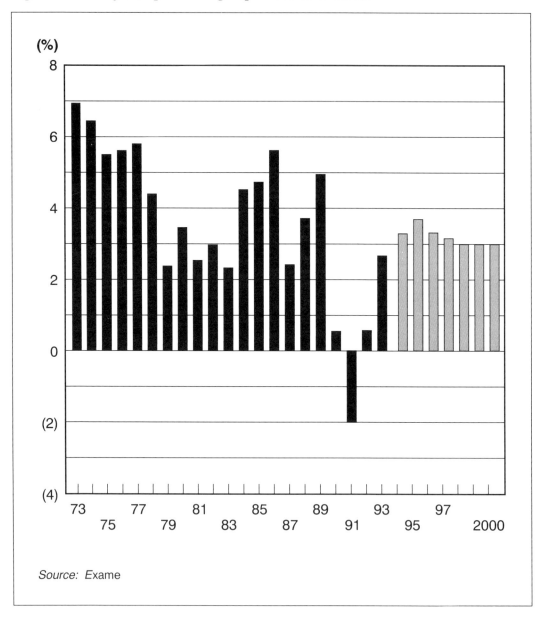

Source: Exame

Profit margins rebound in 1993.

Contrary to popular belief, Brazilian companies are not obsolete. The average age of their equipment is lower than in the U.S. and Europe.

Another issue that requires clarification is obsolescence. Contrary to popular belief, Brazilian companies are not obsolescent. A 1993 survey showed that the average age of their machinery and equipment is around 10.5 years. This compares favorably with 12 years for Europe and 14 years for the U.S. We lose only to the Japanese. After the yen crisis in 1986, they invested massively to modernize their plants and lowered the average age of their equipment to six years. Brazil was at that level in 1986, as a result of massive foreign investments that were flowing in until the early eighties.

We have lost part of our competitive edge and created a technology gap with this 4.5-year increase in the average age of equipment. We have not missed the boat, however. Deterioration of our industry was relative and we have entered the nineties still ahead of the world average.

One of the most positive results of the process of economic liberalization has been technological enhancement, forced by direct competition with foreign products in domestic and foreign markets. In 1990, not a single Brazilian company had an ISO 9000, ISO 9001 or ISO 9002 certificate. Three years later, 600 companies had been certified, placing their products on a par with foreign competition from the quality standpoint. In Argentina, only eight companies had an ISO 9000 certificate at the time.

Many coincidences show that in the early nineties Brazil faces a series of situations similar to those preceding the economic miracle of two decades ago. Some indicators are even better than at the start of the golden age, as we will see in the following pages.

MOVING INTO GEAR FOR A NEW GROWTH CYCLE

- *The Exame 500 resume growth*

- *Slow privatization is no obstacle*

- *Stock exchange boom*

- *The wealthy hinterland*

- *The success of franchising*

- *Popular products, the new avenue for industry*

- *A new entrepreneurial mindset*

In sum, we are witnessing a return to the conditions prevailing in the prosperous seventies, the last time Brazil grew at exponential rates:

- Low international interest rates

- Low levels of corporate debt, as firms ready themselves to start a new cycle of indebtedness and growth

- A return to profitability, and potential reinvestment of 80% of earnings to self-finance growth

- Huge inflows of foreign capital via bank loans and equity markets, as soon as the stabilization program is perceived to have worked

- Greatly improved management and manufacturing quality compared with the run-up to the growth cycle of the seventies.

These are highly favorable conditions for a new surge of growth, which in fact has already started slowly in 1993 and 1994 and will continue until 2005. The top 500 firms share the same expectations of growth. In 1993, 384 leading business organizations resumed growth after the 1990 debacle, when only 71 of the same firms reported sales increases.

The top 500 grew 8.4% in 1993, and a further 11.2% in 1994. Smaller firms, which are more agile, grew 14.2% in 1994, and are set to repeat the performance in 1995. It is true that much of this growth came from regaining sales lost in the 1990 recession and taking up slack capacity, but the momentum is there once again.

A closer analysis of the losses also points to a recovery. In 1991, 249 of the top 500 were in the red, but in 1993 there were only 187 loss makers. In 1993, 80% started showing sales growth and only 30% posted negative year-end results. That was still a high proportion, but it is an acceptable level in the international context. A survey by *Fortune* of the top 500 U.S. companies showed that 19% lost money in 1992 and 1993 (Figure 16).

Figure 16   The top 500 resume growth.

	1987	1988	1989	1990	1991	1992	1993
Sales up	320	316	255	71	226	345	384
Money losers	96	101	70	171	249	165	187
Neg. working capital	143	143	208	236	249	246	254
Multinationals	146	146	147	147	147	147	144

Source: Exame – Melhores e Maiores

Brazilian firms performed noticeably better in 1993.

We now have a globalized economy. Contrary to popular opinion, the international financial community will quickly forget Brazil's 1986 default on its foreign debt and other obstacles cited by those who believe Brazil will never recover its financial credibility. Indeed, before long Brazil will be considered one of the best countries for investment, thanks to its stupendous stock market performance. A booming stock market works wonders for credibility. Instead of losers, we will be seen as winners. Investment bankers and international speculators will earn a lot of money on Brazilian stock exchanges. The first syllable of the word 'speculator' comes from the Latin *speculari*, meaning to look, prospect or examine as in 'spectacle', 'special', 'specialist'. Speculators are in fact people who look ahead, and by doing so make a lot of money and enemies. Although countries are never fond of speculators, or the money they make, Brazil will have to pay a premium to those who put their trust in it before anyone else.

Before long, the talk of the town among Brazil traders in New York will no longer be inflation, Brazil's federal deficit or corruption, but the excellent investment opportunities. International investors will talk about Brazilian equities and about expertly managed Brazilian firms that are booming. Names like Collor, Funaro, or Zelia will be substituted by names like Embraco, Forjas Taurus and TAM Airways, along with those of other efficient businesses. Our image will slowly change for the better. In fact, by the end of 1993 the buzz word on Brazil had already changed from 'over-indebted nation' to 'emerging market', a more positive-sounding term for would-be investors.

Few countries in the world offer so many of the preconditions for rapid growth as Brazil. China and India are two other conspicuous examples.

Whenever the possibility that Brazil is on the verge of a new growth cycle is discussed, potential obstacles are mentioned. Many leading economists are still pessimistic. Roberto Macedo argued in an article in *Estado de S. Paulo* (September 1994) that the latest generation of Brazilians will be poorer than their parents. Roberto Campos predicts in his new 1,400-page book *Lanterna de Proa* that the 'Brazilian dream' will not be achieved by the year 2000. Mario Henrique Simonsen prophesied hyperinflation as recently as February 1994, in a famous article in *Exame* that panicked some readers.

Brazil still faces many problems. My contention is that the positive factors now outnumber the negative factors, and that a virtuous circle is beginning to take effect.

Economists are usually right. Their analysis is correct more often than not; problems and their consequences are accurately expounded; but they are wrong about the order of magnitude. Federal deficits cause inflation. Okay, but how much? State-owned enterprises cause inflation, foreign debt causes inflation. Yes, but what about the magnitude of each and every one of these causes? Many of the problems raised are real enough, but a careful analysis of the figures shows that they have little real effect on the economy.

One of the main negative effects of the public-sector deficit consists of interest payments on short-term government debt. When inflation reigns supreme, no-one holds idle assets or even keeps money in their pockets, since these pay no interest. All available funds are invested in some interest-bearing instrument. Since the Real Plan, demand deposits have surged, and so has the use of cash. Hence the government has effectively reduced its internal debt and interest payments.

In a country that was ruled by the military for 20 years, you might expect military spending to be high. But as a percentage of gross domestic product (GDP) it is only one-fifth of the amount spent by the U.S. on defense.

Another myth: too many employees in government. In fact, Brazil does not have a disproportionate number of public servants, nor are their salaries anything to write home about. Brazil has fewer government employees than the U.K., U.S. or Germany, and most of them are underpaid schoolteachers.

Figure 16A   Military expenditure.

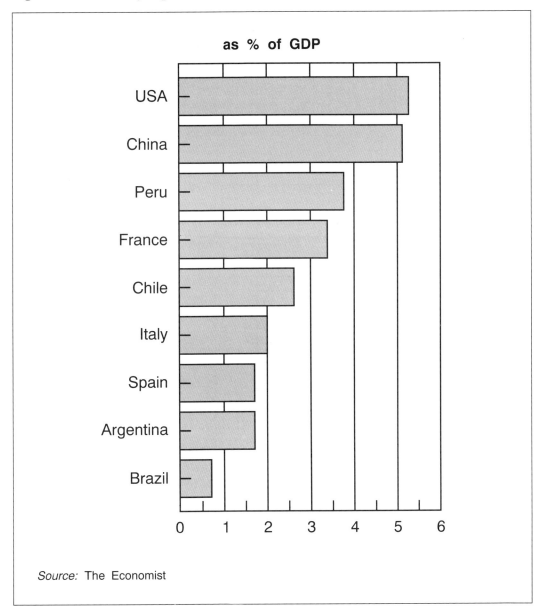

as % of GDP

Source: The Economist

Military expenditures are minimal.

Figure 16B   Public-sector employees.

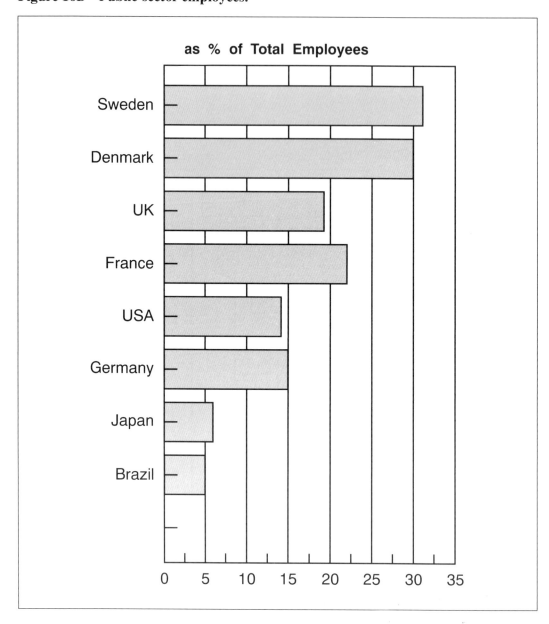

Few public-sector employees.

Privatization is a controversial subject. The slow pace of privatization is frequently viewed as a hindrance to growth. This is a moot point. Take Petrobrás, for example. Loss of its monopoly could boost the oil distribution and refining segments. It would enhance efficiency, and the price of fuel might drop to some extent. However, even the worst-case scenario, i.e. no change in the status of Petrobrás, is not sufficient to prevent a resumption of growth.

President Fernando Henrique Cardoso will probably privatize Vale do Rio Doce (CVRD), the federally-owned mining giant, leaving only two markets controlled or dominated by government: petrochemicals and utilities. And he will press for constitutional reforms to eliminate or at least attenuate the oil and telecoms monopolies, forcing Telebrás and Petrobrás to compete with private enterprise.

In the first place, Petrobrás is already in many ways identical to a private-sector business organization.

It is the private sector that currently finances 70% of Petrobrás's capital needs but without voting rights.

Private investors pension funds and players in the stock market already own over 70% of Petrobrás and most other state-owned enterprises (SOEs). The private sector receives most of the dividends and funds SOEs' growth.

The problem is that most of these outstanding shares do not confer voting rights. Thus the government has a dubious right to control management, since it is established by a law that denies voting rights to thousands of small minority stockholders who own most of the equity. This is hardly commendable from an ethical or democratic point of view, since all stockholders should be given a right to vote.

Nevertheless, Petrobrás is effectively funded by the private sector for at least 70% of its capital needs. The same is true of other SOEs which have a monopoly in areas considered strategic, such as Telebrás. The fact that they are state-owned does not prevent the inflow of private capital into these companies.

Even if these SOEs remain in the hands of a financially weakened government, they will be able to take advantage of the new development cycle, since the private sector will still be funding their investments.

France and Germany have SOEs in the telecoms sector. There are also plenty of French and German advocates of privatization for these SOEs, so as to enhance their efficiency. Yet no-one attempts to argue that this is a necessary condition of development.

In Brazil, the state sector controls only 6% of GNP. It is a mistake to attribute 70% of GNP to SOEs, as some do. SOEs once accounted for a large proportion of the total equity of Brazilian companies, because they operate in capital-intensive sectors such as oil, mining, steel and electricity. However, in effect SOEs retain only 6% of the value added to the economy. Petrobrás controls the oil sector, but since Brazil imports most of its oil, the actual value added is small. Of the 32 industries in the Brazilian economy, the government originally controlled three: steel, public utilities (dozens of countries besides Brazil maintain a state monopoly in this sector), mining, and chemicals and petrochemicals (Figure 17).

With steel mills completely in the hands of private enterprise thanks to the 1990-1993 privatization process, there are now only four sectors under state control.

A successful state-owned enterprise can now be sold for
two or three times the initial capital outlay.

State involvement might even be necessary at start-up, when the risk is high. As soon as the enterprise is consolidated and risk is lower, however, it is time for the entire package to be transferred to private ownership, by auction or flotation and massive dilution of stock among investors and employee. This does not prevent the government from charging a high premium for having put up the money and run the initial risk. A successful SOE can be sold for a price equivalent to two or three times its initial capital.

Figure 17   State ownership in the developed world.

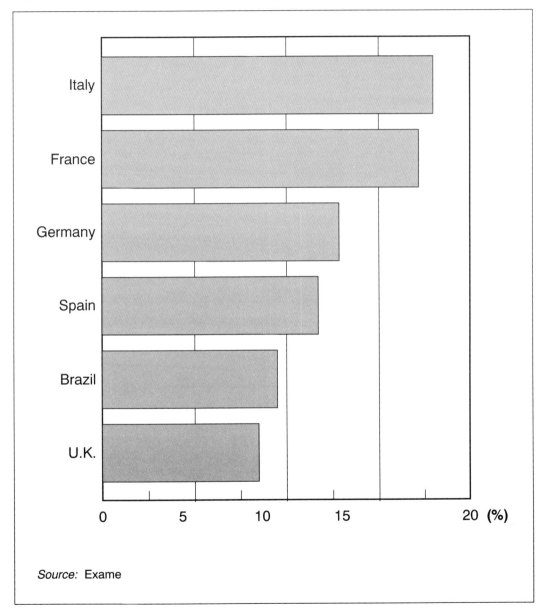

Source: Exame

Contrary to widespread opinion, Brazil has few state-controlled sectors.

Figura 17B   Market share by sector and industry, and percente controlled by local, foreign and state-owned companies.

Sectors	Local Market Share (%)	Foreign Market Share (%)	SOEs' Market Share (%)
Local firms predominate in:			
Agriculture	100	0	0
Construction	100	–	–
Retail	100	–	–
Steel	94	6	–
Fertilizers	91	9	–
Textiles	90	10	–
Paper	81	19	–
Supermarkets	75	25	–
Hotels	74	26	–
Transportation	73	1	26
Electronics	67	33	–
Food	63	37	–
Metalworking	49	44	7
Foreign firms predominate in:			
Automobiles	6	94	–
Household utensils	10	90	–
Pharmaceuticals	23	77	–
Computers	32	67	1
Plastics	41	59	–
Beverages	45	55	–
Machinery	44	56	–
SOEs predominate in:			
Utilities	100	–	–
Mining	31	6	63
Chemicals/ petrochemicals	23	11	66
Source: *Exame*			

Oil was certainly strategic to Brazil during the fifties, when it was important to control the sources of production of this raw material, and Brazil was still totally dependent on imported oil. Petrobrás is now able to produce 50% of domestic needs, and the sector has ceased to be strategic. If a war should interrupt oil supplies, energy conservation and other measures would enable us to survive with 50% of the normal supply. Furthermore, no war lasts forever.

In today's world, it is strategically important to control the communication belt around the earth. Brazil's chances of controlling this system are very slight. We will depend on a system managed by a gigantic consortium of multinational companies in the communications sector. The biggest risk is that the world could declare war on Brazil and block our access to global services, but quite frankly this is a ridiculous hypothesis.

Companies all over the world invest several times the profit made in a year. When you spend more than you earn, you generate a private-sector deficit.

The public-sector deficit is another obstacle to development mentioned by many economists. It is also an issue that deserves more detailed analysis. Brazil will have a public-sector deficit throughout the nineties. It is both intellectually and financially mistaken to consider a balanced budget a prerequisite for growth: no private company operates without a deficit a 'private-sector deficit', as it were. Companies everywhere invest many times the profit they make in a year. The international average is to invest three to four times annual earnings in plant and equipment. When you spend more than your profit, you generate a 'private deficit'.

The question of public and private deficits must be analyzed carefully. They are part of the business world's routine. The main worry is elsewhere: you cannot burden your cash flow with an interest rate in excess of the return you expect from these investments.

In the seventies, Brazilian firms achieved a return of 25% per year, and paid annual interest of 3%. They were investing much more than they could generate in profit and cash flow. But this is an extremely favorable situation. They were simply operating according to the concept of private deficit used by economists in Brazil and elsewhere, by investing more than the profit or cash flow generated.

The real problem is that the Brazilian government does not generate a high return on investment, while paying very high interest rates, set by itself, since it is the biggest borrower of funds.

As you can see, the problem is not having a public-sector deficit, but having poor financial management. We need to improve the rate of return on public investment. The fact is that the Brazilian government has not managed its financial affairs efficiently. It is not even concerned about its image as a financial manager, starting with the Central Bank, which takes no interest in showing that the foreign debt has been eroded, year after year, by U.S. inflation. A good financial manager always allocates part of his promotional funds to improving the organizations's financial image.

It is worth recalling here that Italy has a public-sector deficit equivalent to 12% of GNP; Spain's is 5.2%; Canada's and Britain's are 5%; Sweden's used to be 12%, but is now down to 4.4%. All of these deficits are proportionately bigger than Brazil's, which is 3.2%. Yet these countries do not have inflation rates that come anywhere near Brazil's (Figure 18).

A further problem which usually worries foreign analysts is the national debt. The internal debt of the Brazilian government is not in itself a serious problem. Belgium's national debt is equivalent to 120% of GNP; Italy's is 100%; Canada's is nearly 75%; while in the U.S. it is just under 60%. Despite all the problems and crises it faced in the eighties, in 1992 Brazil's national debt was equivalent to about 35% of GNP (Figures 19 and 20).

Figure 18   Public-sector deficits Brazil and some developed countries (1992).

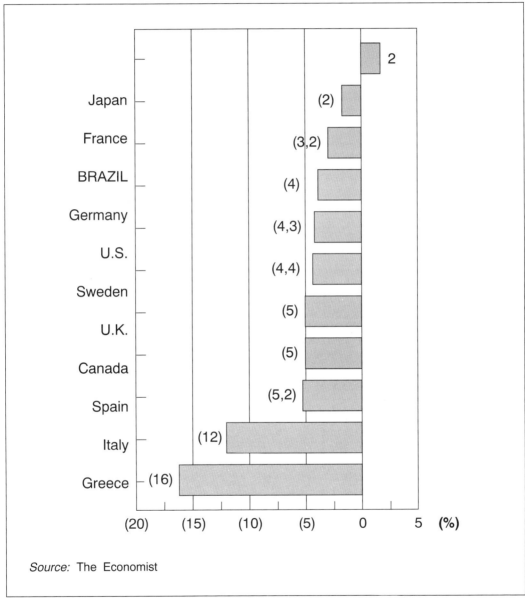

Source: The Economist

In terms of public-sector deficits, Brazil ranks fairly well in the world.

Figure 19   Domestic debt – the national debt as a percentage of GNP.

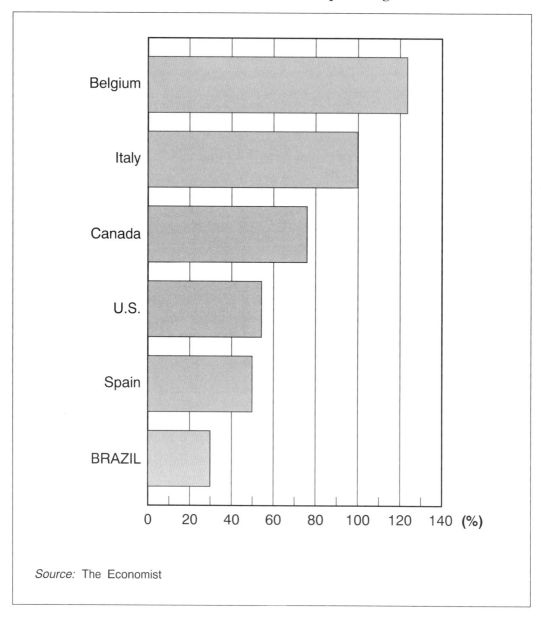

Source: The Economist

Brazil's national debt is small compared to that of other countries.

Figure 20   Competitive advantage – government spending as a percentage of GNP.

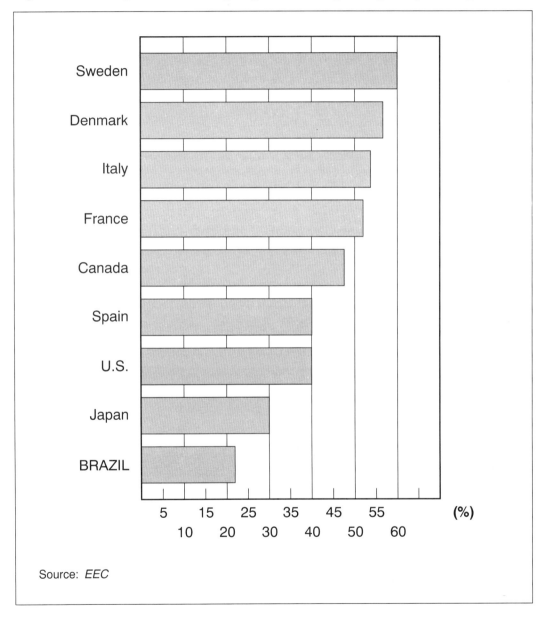

Source: *EEC*

Brazilian government expenditure is relatively small equal to only 25% of GNP.

The problem is the high interest rates paid by government to service its relatively small debt, which confirms that it is a matter of financial management. Only when inflation is curbed will interest rates gradually decrease, for two reasons. First, because without inflationary uncertainty investors will not demand a premium for inflation risk in their short-term loans to the government. Second, when foreign money starts flowing in again, at a 3% real coupon, it will lower the average domestic interest rate.

Domestic interest rates will plummet in 1995-96.

Contrary to popular opinion, there has been no lack of political will to curb inflation in Brazil. Inflation is the nation's and politicians' number one enemy. President José Sarney knew the risk he ran if the Cruzado Plan should fail from the start. A week before the plan was launched, Mr Sarney requested that the island of Fernando de Noronha be made ready for a strategic withdrawal. He was convinced that he would have to resign in disgrace if the plan failed during its first week.

The day before announcement of the Cruzado Plan, no-one knew for sure whether it would work. No-one could foresee the reactions of bankers and the population, or whether hyperinflation would break out on the following day. President Sarney knew that tackling inflation carried a high political risk. Later, Mr Collor was to act the same way, placing all his chips on a gamble against inflation in his very first political action.

Innumerable other government initiatives in the fight against inflation should induce us to rethink the view that politicians have done nothing to solve the nation's biggest economic problem. Politicians voted in all the plans, even that of Mr Collor who, unlike Mr Sarney, did not have majority support in Congress. The legislators had to rewrite several anti-inflation laws and measures submitted by the Executive, to eliminate a welter of conceptual and legal errors. Four or five government economists, with no experience in business or practical affairs, would secretly concoct a plan with very little outside help. Past plans failed owing to technical problems, rather than a lack of political will.

Over the past 20 years or so, more than 200 U.S.-trained economists have worked for government. They got their doctoral degrees in economics at Yale, Chicago and Harvard. During the same period only one Harvard MBA has been recruited by Brasília.

Success is in the details, not the grandiosity of the plan.

A key problem with the Cruzado Plan was overlooking the fact that industrial goods were sold with a 30-day credit period and producer prices therefore included a 16% expected inflation rate. When prices were frozen they still had this built-in component to compensate for future inflation, playing havoc with the pricing system. In March 1986, the Brazilian economy stood still for a full month while suppliers and customers quarreled over the deflation factor to be used. None of the 18 authors of the Cruzado Plan had stopped to think about this small detail. This oversight gave rise to the joke that none of the 'Crusaders' had ever written an IOU in their entire lives.

I mention all this to counter the conventional wisdom that most inflation plans fail for lack of political will, or because economists are bereft of the support of politicians, who destroy their plans for electoral gains. The truth is that most plans have been half-baked and full of conceptual flaws. Economists tend to blame politicians for their failures instead of blaming themselves.

The Real Plan learned from many of these mistakes. The Real Plan was by far the most simple and the most effective way to curb inflation.

Changes in the constitution are not necessary. The modern world is not run from the top down but from the bottom up.

The results of the Real Plan are already in, and they are positive. The Real Plan has completed its cycle, from beginning to end, and inflation has effectively been subdued. The problem is to avoid new inflation, not to prevent the old inflation from resurging, as in Mexico and Argentina. Technically speaking, they are two different animals.

This follow-up problem occurred with Argentina's Cavallo Plan. The program was well planned at the start, but a year later Argentina had an exchange-rate lag of 18%-25% (depending on how you do your sums), and the economy was virtually at a standstill, giving rise to severe social problems.

Figure 20A   Argentina's plan is different.

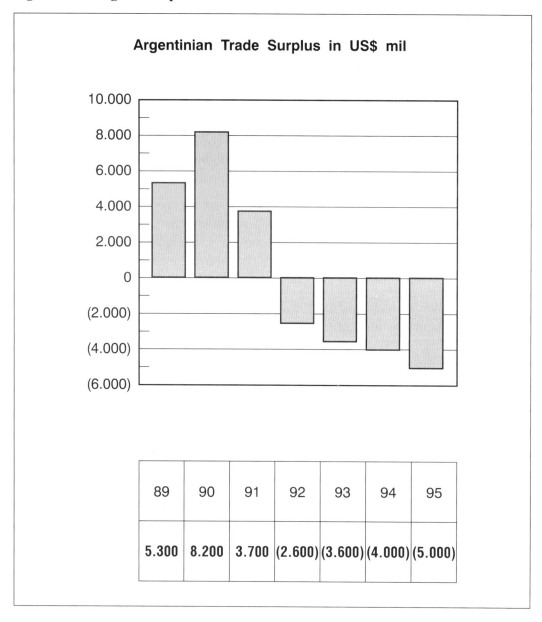

Trade deficit problem to solve.

The Cavallo Plan has not yet reached its conclusion, which theoretically will occur when the exchange rate is free to float again. Brazil has already switched to a new local currency, bringing its program to completion. There is nothing artificial in the Brazilian economy at this moment, leaving big problems to be faced one day. Prices, wages and exchange rates are already freely determined by the market.

It is often argued that Brazil will not modernize or resume growth until several key sections of the constitution are rewritten. Others believe that no constitutional amendments are necessary. If we look at this question in broader perspective, we will see that the modern world is not run from the top down but from the bottom up. The constitution and the many amendments already made no longer have much influence on the direction society will take. Constitutionally, bank interest rates are limited to 12% per year, but this does not prevent the Central Bank from systematically 'breaking the law' by setting rates up to three times that ceiling.

The 1988 constitutional reform decentralized government, a positive and constructive move. The objection raised by federal government economists and former finance ministers at the time was that tax revenues were decentralized without a decentralization of government obligations, thereby generating a negative cash flow. Thus many economists advocate a tax reform so that the federal government can regain the revenues it has lost to state and municipal governments.

Fortunately, that will not be President Cardoso's policy. In his election platform entitled 'Back To Work', the main thrust is the idea of delegating to state and municipal governments the responsibility for many services previously provided by the federal government. That is much more cost-efficient and cost-effective than continuing to have centralized provision by the federal government.

Congress is right of center. It always has been, even if some speeches sound left-wing. Most political analysts in the 1994 presidential election were led astray by initial polls that gave the far-left candidate, Luís Ignácio Lula da Silva of the Workers' Party, a 42% lead.

This percentage should more accurately be termed a notoriety index: Lula was the only well-known candidate for a long time. Most voters (67%) were uncommitted early on in the campaign. The exceptions were mainly hard-core militants of the Workers' Party. Lula never really won the support of more than 25% of the electorate.

Figure 20B   Congress is right of center.

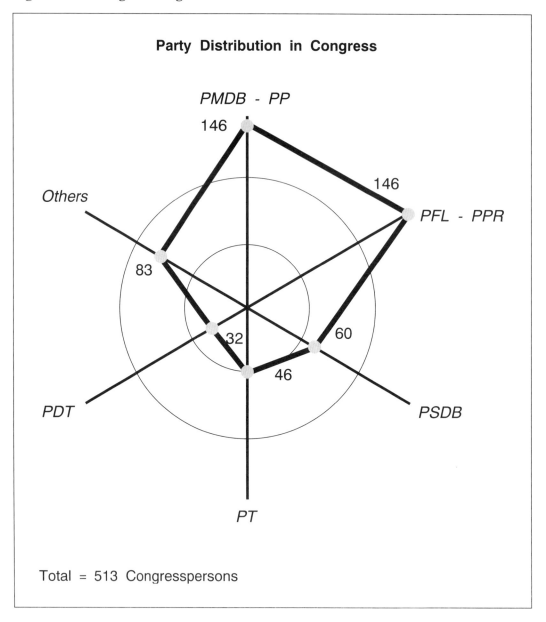

Party Distribution in Congress

PMDB - PP

146

146

PFL - PPR

Others

83

32   60

46

PDT

PSDB

PT

Total = 513 Congresspersons

A left-wing party is necessary in a country with as many poor citizens as Brazil has. Unfortunately the Workers' Party has old-fashioned views on management, organization, and the need to increase productivity. It is a question of ways and means, not of objectives.

Contrary to conventional wisdom, the number of strikes in Brazil is extremely low. Fewer days are lost to industrial stoppages than in Italy, Spain, France or Portugal. Brazilian labor leaders are less politically motivated and more interested in economic demands than most people realize.

Vicentinho, a prominent union leader, told *Exame*, Brazil's leading business magazine, that the prevailing attitude in the labor movement is to talk first and strike as a last resort. Ten years ago, the attitude was exactly the opposite: strike first, talk later.

Our best MBAs are working for multinational companies rather than for government. Most multinationals forbid their trusted executives to engage in political activities. This is an unfortunate mistake. Senior managers are precisely the kind of people who could contribute most to the elimination of poverty in Brazil. The notion that multinationals must not meddle in another countries' affairs has to change. The involvement could be direct or through philanthropy, which is currently non-existent.

Brazil has a first-class management elite, seasoned by a hostile and volatile environment. With the end of inflation, they are finally finding enough time to focus on issues that relate to growth instead of protecting their companies from inflation.

This time around, the economy will be driven by different forces than in the past, when growth was government-induced. This time growth will be business-centered, driven by decisions made by the top 500 corporations, by small firms, and by young entrepreneurs who are setting up franchises all over the country. The important thing is not a vast comprehensive economic policy but the managerial efficiency of thousands of small and medium businesses. If these people do their job badly, Brazil will not make progress. If the grand economic program is a flop, if the constitution leaves much to be desired, the effect will not be the same as 40 years ago, when the world was more authoritarian, governments held sway, and force was exerted from the top down.

Figure 20C   Comparative advantage: few industrial stoppages.

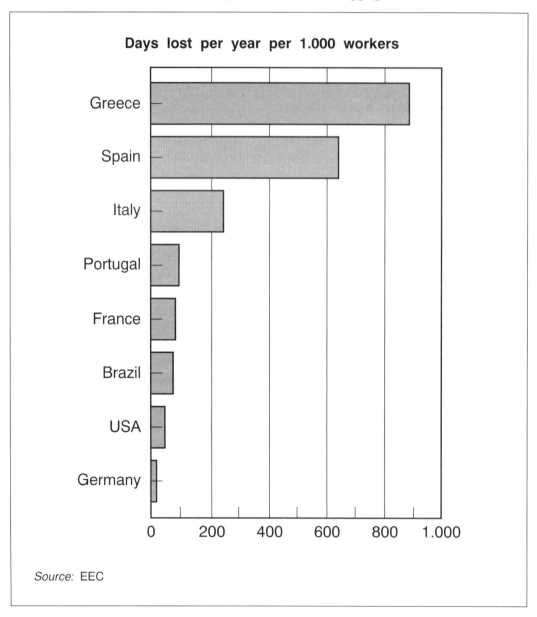

Few strikes in Brazil.

Economic growth in itself will overcome many
of Brazil's deficiencies.

The analysis presented up to this point leads to the conclusion that the balance is positive. Growth in itself will help overcome most of Brazil's deficiencies, especially its huge social debt. It is easier to steer a truck when it is moving than when it is standing still.

A resumption of growth increases government spending
power without raising taxes.

The financing is there, the ability to take out more financing is there, but will there be available income to support the new growth cycle expected for the next ten years, since there is no growth without consumption? It is no use investing billions of dollars in the Brazilian economy if the population does not have the income to spend so that the wealth generated can spread. A close look at some indicators in this area shows that purchasing power is set to rise.

The first positive aspect is the changing profile of the population. In the seventies and eighties, Brazilians started to control the size of their families, and fertility steadily declined. From 6.2 children per woman in 1960, it dropped to 4.5 in the early seventies, and 3.0 in the early nineties. Projections indicate a further slide to 2.3 or 2.4 by the end of the century. At that level, Brazil will be just above the European average, 1.8 children per woman (Figure 21).

Figure 21   Fertility rate falls.

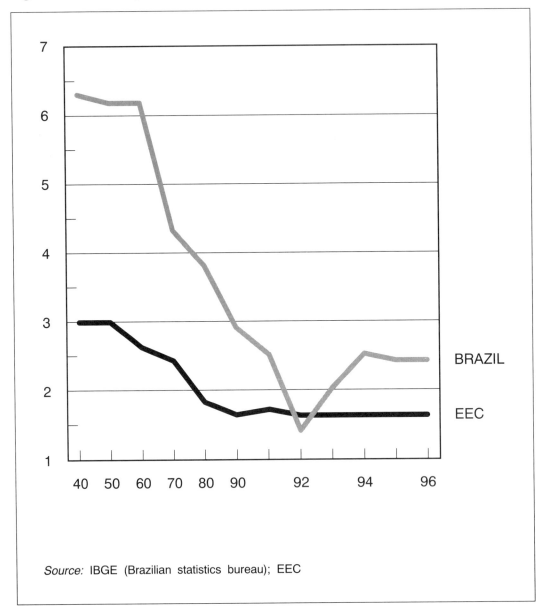

Source: IBGE (Brazilian statistics bureau); EEC

The threat of overpopulation has not materialized in Brazil. The number of children per family is steadily decreasing.

A brutal recession in 1992 pushed down the fertility rate to 1.4 per woman, the lowest rate ever recorded in the country. Couples were postponing marriage, and those who did marry were postponing their first child. This, of course, is a temporary statistic; as soon as growth resumes, the fertility rate should go back up to 2.5 children per woman.

New consumers to challenge marketing strategies: Dinks, the double-income no-kids household, with money to spare.

Figures indicate that Brazil has solved one of its most serious problems. The threat of an uncontrollable population explosion that loomed at the end of the fifties did not materialize. Instead, the fertility rate has dropped.

The 1992 recession ushered in a new consumer, already familiar to other countries: the Dinks, dual income no kids. Husband and wife both work, earn more than older couples, delay their first child, and have more money to spend. This new model challenges the creativity of marketing departments and advertising agencies.

Falling fertility rates mean an aging population. But in the Brazilian case that is excellent news, unlike those where aging becomes a pressing economic problem. Families reach their yearly maximum spending budget by the age of 40, when the children go to college. After 40, it is all down hill, at least from a financial point of view.

The average age in the U.S. and Japan is slowly approaching the 40s. In Brazil the average age is 23. These youngsters are just beginning to spend and earn. They are not yet highly productive, which also comes with age. In terms of a spending curve, Brazil is still on the uphill side. No direct analogy can be drawn, of course, between an average and the entire population, but the general direction is the same.

Figure 21A   An aging population is good news.

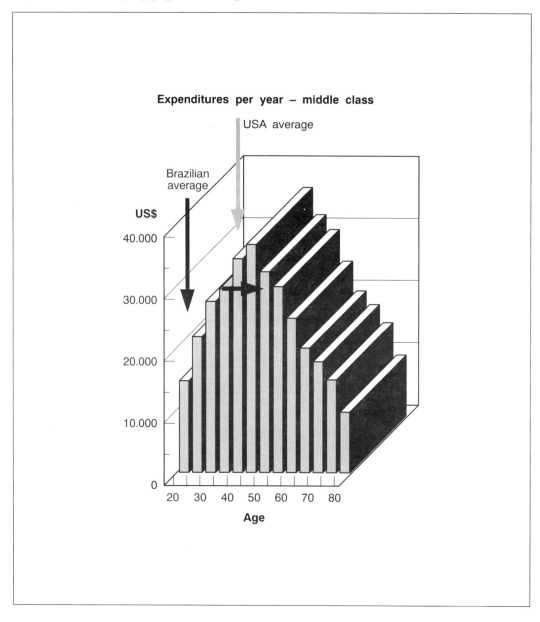

Brazilians are begining their expenditure life cicle.

Another important social change, to be discussed below, is the franchising movement, which entails an inversion in traditional migratory flows. In the past, migrants have always gone in search of success in the big city. Today educated young people, born in the big cities, are heading to smaller towns in the hinterland to set up a business and promote a true revolution in local consumer habits. That means more disposable income in regional markets.

Another significant social phenomenon that took place in the seventies was a massive increase in the number of women entering the job market. The traditional family in which the husband was the only breadwinner was replaced by the working couple. From that point on, women became a new and important source of income for the family. This translates into even more disposable income, a trend that is still in the making (Figure 22).

The end of inflation spells a halt to profiteering from inflation by banks. A two-day float with inflation running at 2% per day is a banker's dream. This is the meaning of a transaction that takes a day to be debited to a customer's account, a deposit that takes three days to be credited to a branch in the Northeast, or a full week in Manaus. For the majority of the population, it led to losses that are estimated to have reached US$35 billion a year, for inflation of approximately 45% per month.

This dividend of low inflation is already achieving concrete effects. The lower-income strata have enjoyed a surge in disposable income simply because inflation has ended. The stupendous potential for growth in low-price markets will be discussed in a later section.

There is US$12 billion in paper money stuffed inside the mattresses of the Brazilian middle class.

Because of the 'lost decade' and producers' flight from expensive credit, the loan volume of the average Brazilian bank is extremely low only four times its capital, compared with a historical average of 12 times. Brazilian banks can now triple their loan base without jeopardizing their own financial health or the health of the entire financial system.

Figure 22   Women enter the labor market.

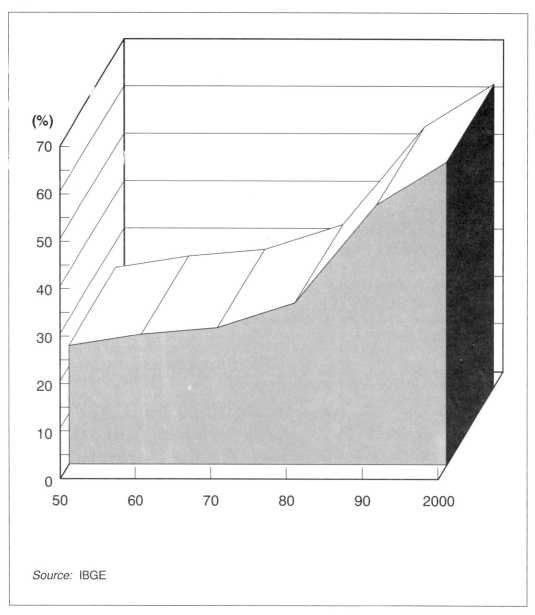

Source: IBGE

In the year 2000, 70% of productive women will be in the job market.

Banks' every effort during the eighties focused on making money from inflation. They offered services of various kinds free of charge to attract deposits, because that was how banks made money. The end of inflation will shift banks' day-to-day operations toward attracting borrowers and making loans.

The positive side of the excessive profit that banks got away with in the past is that reinvestment of this profit has increased the extremely solid capital base banks already had. This will bring an added momentum to the economy in the coming phase.

Furthermore, the volume of consumer credit is set to expand tenfold, a potent fuel to keep the economy growing until the year 2005.

High inflation rates gave rise to a habit of saving in U.S. dollars, literally stuffed into the mattress. A research study by Nena Gerusa Cei at the University of São Paulo estimated that middle-class families kept some US$12 billion in the home as a reserve for lean years. These were dollar bills, genuine greenbacks, supplied by black market dealers at an average of US$5,000 per family, reaching as much as US$100,000 in some instances.

Of course, there will always be money under the mattress, but with the improvement of the economy a significant portion of this reserve will end up being spent. After all, there is little need to hold savings in this form during fat years.

In my view, these savings were largely responsible for the 1993 boom in car sales. The auto industry's domestic performance that year far exceeded the rise in disposable income in the period. The increase in sales was certainly driven by savings, mattress dollars among them. The incentive to spend savings on cars arose from an agreement between the auto industry and government to pass along tax cuts to consumers.

When Americans invest in Brazil, it is called strategic diversification, i.e. not putting all your eggs in one basket. When Brazilians invest abroad, the *Financial Times* and *Wall Street Journal* mutter about capital flight. Brazilian investments abroad total between US$60 billion and US$90 billion. The U.S. government has set up tax-free zones to attract funds from Latin America, which otherwise would be taxed at 25% to 35% in their home countries. Financial dumping through tax incentives has created what is erroneously called flight capital.

Now that U.S. interest rates are relatively low again, I suspect that US$30 billion-US$45 billion will return to Brazil, either as direct investment or through the stock market under Annex 4. Home building is a nifty way to get money back into the country, and a construction boom will probably be fueled by this money as it is repatriated.

The stock exchange boom works wonders for the investment climate. The effect eventually diffuses to the entire business climate.

Pessimists will worry at this point about a likely resurgence of inflationary pressures originating in production so-called cost-push inflation. This possibility exists because the nation has not prepared as it should for a new surge in growth. Fortunately, however, imports can make up for possible shortfalls in supply. If there is a steel shortage, for instance, we can import steel instead of raising the price, as in the seventies.

One more source of disposable income when growth resumes will be profit taking in the stock market. The main stock index, operated by Bovespa (the São Paulo Stock Exchange), will double or even triple in the next two years. There will be a new period of euphoria very similar to 1971, when companies took advantage of the stock exchange boom to go public. The result was ten years of poor stock market performance as one company after another floated 49% of its capital.

This problem will not recur because most companies have already gone public, and since Brazilians like to keep control over their business, there will not be a flood of new issues. The pace at which companies go to the stock market to raise capital will not be as hectic as in 1971, because the level of corporate debt is now very low, and there is therefore no pressing need to boost capital inflows. New issues will not dry up, evidently; they will simply proceed at a normal pace.

This scenario means several years of growth and high performance for equities. Many investors will choose profit taking and undoubtedly channel some of their gains towards consumption besides other types of investment.

A bullish stock market works wonders for the general mood of business executives and ends up spreading to the economy as a whole. The Brazilian stock market is still playing the value game, seeking grossly undervalued shares. As the economy starts picking up steam, the value game will be substituted by the growth stock game.

At present (November 1994), the average price/earnings ratio in Brazil is around 7, whereas in most emerging markets the average is around 25. As the average P/E ratio in Brazil rises to normal levels, there is room for the market to triple. Add to that the positive effect of the increased profits generated by economic growth, and it could double again in the next seven years. In view of all these positive factors combined, the stock market may well grow sixfold in a period of ten years, provided economic growth and stability are maintained (Figures 23, 24 and 25).

One of the fastest-moving businesses in the next few years will be mergers and acquisitions (M&A). Many a family-owned business is up for sale, just waiting for company prices to rise to what they were in 1986. A study by Price Waterhouse shows not only that the M&A market is already exploding, but that foreign buyers are now 45% of the takers and will swiftly become the major players.

New management methods introduced in the construction industry have enhanced efficiency and reduced waste, thereby cutting costs in half. Housing has a significant weight in family budgets: a lower-middle-class family spends up to 25% of its income on this item. The reduction in building costs will enable families to allocate a smaller portion of their income to housing, thus leaving more for consumption of other items.

Part of this extra disposable income will of course be spent on bigger, more expensive homes. This too will feed into the construction market, since standards will be raised. During the lost decade, the average size of a three-bedroom apartment practically halved. In the next ten years the average size of homes should double, thus returning to the average size that was standard in the 70s.

Figure 23   Equities market set to expand.

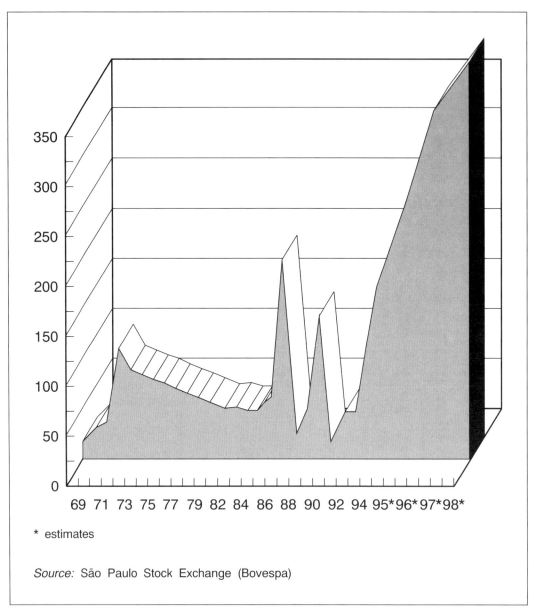

* estimates

Source: São Paulo Stock Exchange (Bovespa)

A euphoric climate stimulates business throughout the economy.

Figure 24   Stocks are still cheap in Brazil.

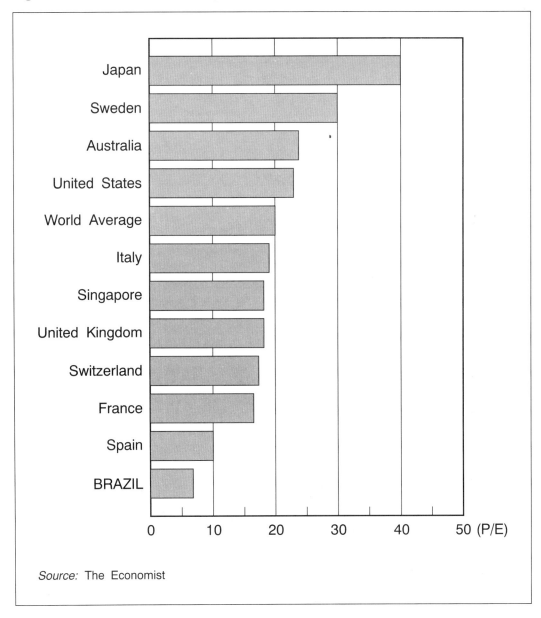

Source: The Economist

The price/earnings (P/E) ratios of Brazilian stocks are set to rise to 30, and profits to double, in the next ten years.

Figure 25A   Foreigners in stock exchanges – participation in the spot market.

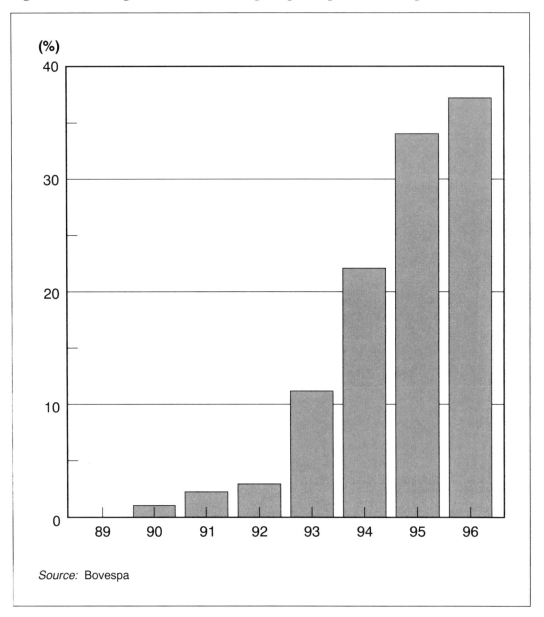

Source: Bovespa

Foreign investment will account for 35% of daily trading volume in stock exchanges.

Figure 25B   Mergers and acquisitions.

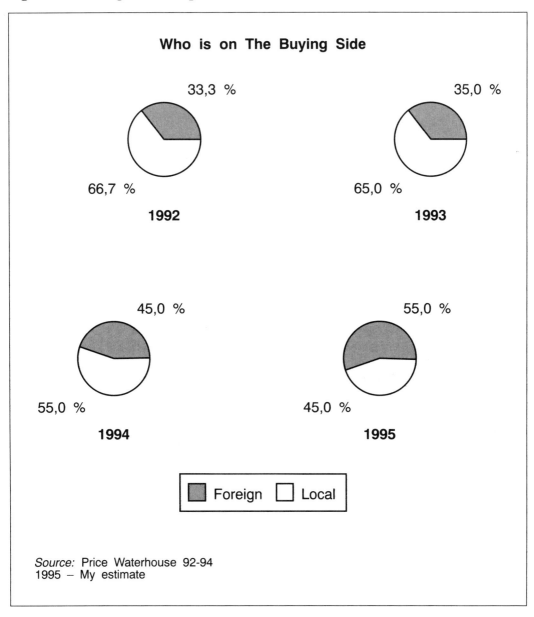

M&A will be very activate.

***Educated young people born in the big cities are moving to small towns,
taking money, talent and promising businesses with them.
The westward movement has begun.***

Of all the socio-economic transformations that took place in Brazil during the recessive eighties, the most fascinating of all, without a doubt, was the move away from big cities. Over the last 200 years of its history, Brazil became accustomed to hearing success stories about young people who left home towns in rural São Paulo, Minas Gerais, or Pernambuco, attracted to the big cities in search of fame and fortune. That was good for them but bad for their home towns, which lost entrepreneurial talent, and disastrous for distribution of income, which ended up concentrated in big cities.

In the nineties, however, it has become more and more commonplace for young people born to wealthy, long-established families in big cities, and educated at prestigious universities, to move in the opposite direction, taking up residence in the interior. They take with them money, talent, promising businesses, and even more important, entrepreneurship.

From 1988 to 1993, over 50,000 franchises started operating, and nine out of ten were successful. Brazil now ranks third in the franchising industry worldwide, after the United States and Japan. In 1994 there were 230 shopping centers and malls under construction in Brazil to house thousands of new franchise stores, especially in the fast-food and garment sectors. Certain franchises are found in every major city in the country (Figure 26).

Franchising has had a fantastic effect on the development of entrepreneurship all over Brazil, and it propagates modern management techniques among the general population. It is a safe business because it holds no secrets for the franchisee; the franchisor has every interest in supplying all necessary support.

The entrepreneur, therefore, feels amply supported when he moves to a small town. The franchisor delivers the business with its accounting system in place and with structured management techniques, enabling the franchisee to devote his energy to addressing key business issues, such as how to attract customers, and even to serving them personally because he can avoid getting bogged down in the bureaucratic part of the business.

Figure 26   Franchising – the wealth of small-town Brazil.

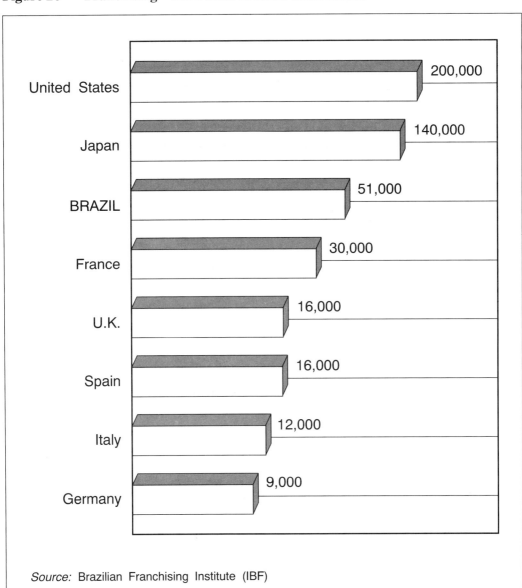

Source: Brazilian Franchising Institute (IBF)

Brazil ranks third worldwide in terms of the number of franchises.

In the seventies, many a jobless engineer opened a juice stall on Avenida Paulista in São Paulo or the like (indeed, this was the theme of a successful movie). In contrast, the present generation have the chance of becoming successful franchisees.

When multinationals in Brazil were downsizing, they gave generous handshakes to the personnel laid off. Most of these highly skilled employees received severance payments of between US$100,000 and US$200,000. Many used the money to set up a franchise, which they now operate.

Experience shows that an engineer who goes to live in a smaller town does not content himself with his first franchise, but sets up other, bolder businesses later on. While big cities suffer from hectic traffic, violence and other stress-generating problems, small-town Brazil receives the benefit of comfort and leisure characteristic of big cities without losing its quality of life. Disposable income increases dramatically in small towns since practically every household expense is lower.

This flow of competent people reverses the historical trend of migration to the big cities. Wealth in rural areas will no longer be generated by farming alone. The increase in productivity driven by this enterprise spirit also means a boost to the national income from regions that are relatively remote from the big urban centers. Another increase in disposable income.

Of every 100 franchises opened, 86% are successful. The move to small towns is permanent.

Thanks to franchising, we will not waste money, time and talent as the English and Americans did during the 19th-century cycle of industrial development, when four out of every five small concerns closed their doors in the first five years of operation. The ratio still prevails even today in those countries, because well-meaning people who start a business without taking advantage of the franchising system will fall into a trial-and-error curve, with a failure rate of around 80% in the first five years of operation.

In present-day Brazil, out of every ten engineers, architects, lawyers and other professionals or executives who lost their jobs in the harsh downsizing process and moved to small towns to make a fresh start, nine will succeed. According to a study on franchising that I coordinated as a follow-up to a survey I have been conducting for *Exame* for the last five years, 86% of new franchises are successful.

Curiously enough, franchising is solving another Brazilian problem: education. Franchising will serve as a training experience for good managers of small businesses and for entrepreneurs. Our business schools train fine executives for the top 500 corporations, but they are still not able to prepare competent people to start up new businesses.

The three-month intensive training given by McDonald's makes a good franchise manager a professional ready to open another franchise, or to establish his own business in some other sector. The young people of the nineties want to succeed from the start of their career. With that objective in mind they seek more efficiency and are concerned about administrative and management matters, so as to achieve their goals more quickly.

The westward movement has only just begun. The interior will be the greatest growth market of all. During the next ten years there will be an industrial and commercial revolution in the hinterland, supplementing the income from agriculture.

That will be the end of the export-centered policies of the eighties, since the local currency will cease to be undervalued as it was then. Given that the debt problem has been solved, generating massive exports will not be a priority. Interest rates are also down, further reducing the need for huge trade surpluses in emerging nations. No need for incentives and dumping: commodity prices will start to rally, and the increase in commodity prices will compensate for appreciation of the currency. Since the inception of the Real Plan, the currency has appreciated 15%.

Brazil will continue to export, but the main thrust will definitely be toward the domestic market. Brazil has never exported more than 8% of its GDP, a relatively small proportion compared to the Asian tigers. But they are no model for a country like Brazil. We are much more similar to the U.S. in size and diversity, and the U.S. has never been an export-driven economy.

Figure 26   Exports and GDP – the end of export-driven policies.

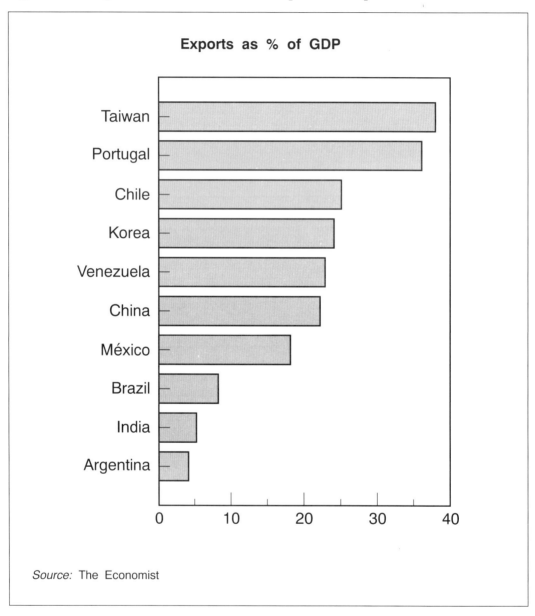

Source: The Economist

Reduction in exports does not hurt Brazil.

You can see the entrepreneurial revolution in Brazil the moment you get off the plane and enter the airport bookstore. In the early seventies, fewer than ten books on business administration were translated and published every year in Brazil. In 1993, as many as 150 new books on business were published, by Brazilians or in translation. Even philosophical discussions such as *Relevance Lost* have been translated, not to mention all of Michael Porter's books.

There are no official statistics on sales of these books, but estimates indicate that between 700,000 and 1.3 million books on business are sold per year in Brazil. I myself am one of the authors of an accounting textbook which has already sold half a million copies, an impressive number even in America. The number of students seeking business administration courses escalates yearly.

In 1976, *Fortune* published a special article on the Harvard Business School class of '46. The magazine followed these students' careers and found out that 50% had become the president of one of the top 500 U.S. companies. The other half had started their own businesses, some of which ended up among those top 500. A successful class, no doubt.

Exame did a similar survey of the Getúlio Vargas Foundation (FGV) class of '56. This was the first class to graduate from FGV's business administration course, which at that time had professors from the prestigious University of Michigan. The survey of these graduates' careers showed that 98% ended up as managers or directors of multinationals, one joined the FGV faculty and only one started his own firm, which is not among the top 500 Brazilian companies.

A 1994 survey by an FGV professor found that 98% of his students expected to open their own business in ten years' time a radical change of attitude in relation to the school's first graduate class.

The new entrepreneurial frame of mind has taken root in the country's business schools, which instead of training managers for multinationals are becoming incubators of new businesses. The University of São Paulo and FGV already offer courses on small business administration. One of the best-selling books on business by a Brazilian author is *O Empreendedor* ('The Entrepreneur'), by Ronald Degen, a professor at FGV.

***Companies will be in trouble if they wait to follow the government's lead
instead of finding their own way.***

The new business mindset that is crystallizing is based on the knowledge that the world no longer grows from the top down but from the bottom up. Companies will be in trouble if they wait to follow the government's lead, as they usually did in the past. The successful companies are those that have turned their backs on government, and have given up waiting and bargaining for loans, financing and fiscal incentives.

Construtora Rossi of São Paulo, for instance, could not obtain sufficient loans from Caixa Econômica Federal (the national savings and home loans bank) to finance its building projects. It solved its problems by developing a financing plan of its own. By means of an elaborate financial engineering scheme, the company launched a '100-Month Plan' to finance the sale of apartments directly to buyers in 100 installments with no government backing.

The view that Brazil is a large orchestra conducted preferably by the finance minister is obsolete. I prefer the image of a country made up of thousands of musical groups of the most diverse styles. Some play rock 'n roll, some play pop, some play chamber music. Each plays its own tune, not under a single conductor's baton, but trying to please its own audience, the customers. The management keynote is to keep an eye out for the customer, not the finance minister.

Brazil has suffered a great deal from the economists' view of the future. I know dozens of business people who hired economic advisors, paying their weight in gold, to find out ahead of time what would happen to the economy, interest rates and inflation. Modern enterprises do not try to foresee the future; they decide to create their own future.

In the business world, stories abound of visionaries who could not make it, owing to either technical or managerial incompetence. No successful businessman or businesswoman tries to predict the future; he or she makes it.

Understandably, most Brazilian companies used to concentrate on trying to predict the future, so as to defend themselves from the next half-baked economic plan. There was no room for strategic planning in an inflationary environment. Brazil has more than 5,000 PhDs in inflationary policy, but fewer than 100 MBAs in corporate planning and growth-related issues.

It is no coincidence that Japan and Germany were the most successful countries of the post-war period. Both were economically ruined and had only one option open to them: to establish the future that was to be attained and make the whole nation strive tirelessly to attain it.

Here we have two completely different conceptions: there are countries that attempt to predict the bad things the future has in store and to defend themselves, and countries that define their own future and know what they want to accomplish.

The reign of the economist in Brazilian government is over. The end of inflation coincided with four finance ministers in a row who were not economists (Messrs Resende, Cardoso, Ricupero, and Gomes).

There is a new Protestant ethic brewing slowly in Brazilian society. Over the last 30 years, the Catholic church has lost market share continuously to Protestants and other religions based on a work ethic, that value profit without rejecting donations – and do not consider it a sin to make money, especially if part of it is sent to the address shown at the bottom of the TV screen.

Until 1993 the only Brazilian prize for business excellence was awarded by *Exame*, through its yearbook *Melhores e Maiores* ('Best and Biggest'). I set up this award 21 years ago, based on a survey of the best business practices in Brazil. We were ten years ahead of Tom Peters and his classic *In Search of Excellence*, but unfortunately we wrote in Portuguese and published in Brazil. Right idea, wrong country.

Two years ago, the Brazilian government instituted a National Quality Prize, similar the U.S.'s Malcolm Baldrige Award. The first year, the award went to IBM. This would have been unacceptable in the seventies because IBM is a multinational. The second time around, in 1994, the prize went to Xerox, another foreign subsidiary. This shows an amazing change of attitude on the part of the Brazilian government.

History repeats itself, but never in quite the same way. Marketing departments will no longer target the richest 10%.

It may be somewhat premature to state that Brazil has regained its vocation for attaining developed-country status. We have lost our competitive edge over the Asian countries, which did not have to cope with foreign debt or the problems of the 'lost decade'.

I do not espouse the thesis, put forward by so many people, that the next surge of growth will be export-led. My feeling is that the driving force will be the new industrial areas that are springing up in Ceará, Santa Catarina, Minas Gerais and São Paulo, away from the traditional centers of the national economy. Brazil has an enormous domestic market at its disposal, and therefore does not have to follow export-driven economic policies like those of the Asian tigers or Chile.

History repeats itself, but never in quite the same way. Obviously many things will have to be done differently from the way they were done in the seventies. For example, international banks will not lend to Brazil as they did in the seventies, simply because the lending limits imposed by most central banks to this day take no account of the effect of inflation on their currencies. Brazilian companies will have to depend on foreign pension funds, and many have no tradition in that area. Firms are slowly adapting, even taking road shows around the world, but it is a process that takes time.

One of the most important changes will relate to corporate strategy. The prevailing strategy in Brazil has focused on producing for the richest 10% of the population. In the seventies, industrial policy consisted basically of import substitution. Brazil started to produce products that had hitherto been imported, usually by the wealthiest, with technology and a degree of sophistication that made them very remote from the average consumer.

Since many companies were subsidiaries of multinationals, most of them simply began producing locally the same products manufactured by the parent company in the U.S., German or Japan headquarters. In other words, the products were totally inappropriate to the low average income of Brazilians.

The focus on producing goods and services suitable to the developed world parallels the culture conveyed in most books on management by foreign authors, who focus on ideas suited to their respective home countries. Brazil began making antilock brake systems (ABS), Dolby stereo sets, shopping malls paved with marble, auto-reversing tape decks and other sophisticated items that matter to the American consumer, but are of questionable priority to Brazilians.

The new Brazilian industrial model will focus on marketing to low-income families. The number of rich people is decreasing.

The winning corporate strategy will target the low-income family. This market must have the highest growth potential in Brazil. The strategy of selling to the wealthiest 10% will no longer be successful, because the number of rich people is decreasing, and also because thanks to trade liberalization they will prefer to import, as they have traditionally done in the past.

Furthermore, Brazilian industry is incapable of producing high-tech goods, or competing with imported products, simply because the number of rich people in Brazil is very small compared with the U.S., Europe and Japan.

The difference between consumer markets in Brazil and the developed world becomes clearer when we compare a car worker at a General Motors plant in Brazil, producing de luxe Omegas year after year without the slightest chance of buying one, with a mechanic who works at BMW in Germany and drives to work in his own BMW, even if it is a second-hand one.

As a user of the car he manufactures, the German worker develops a more critical relationship with the article he produces during his daily routine. The slightest noise in the rear suspension while driving leads this worker to participate in efforts to improve the vehicle's quality. He will certainly exchange ideas with supervisors on ways of enhancing product quality from then on. In less than a week the problem may have been solved and the product improved without top management ever having heard about the matter.

An analogous situation in Brazil is as follows. Only after dozens of dissatisfied consumers have complained to the dealers who supplied their cars will dealerships take the problem to the marketing director, who will then talk to the production director. Depending on the auto maker's celerity, it will then take from six months to a year to solve the problem.

In his book The *Competitive Advantage of Nations*, Michael Porter clearly shows that no company can win the competitive struggle unless it has demanding customers. One of the reasons for Japan's success is the extremely demanding Japanese consumer. In Japan, stores and supermarkets are open on Sundays so that their consumers will have more time to make comparisons between products.

***We must take the ABS out of the brakes, take the Dolby out of stereo systems,
take the auto-reverse button out of tape decks, and build malls without marble.***

In this context, Brazilian industry will obviously never be able to make products for the higher income brackets as competently and efficiently as companies in the developed world. Our industry must adapt production to the prevailing income level less sophisticated products are more suited to local conditions. We need to take the ABS out of the brakes, take the Dolby out of the stereo systems, take the auto-reverse button away from tape decks, and build malls with no marble.

The commitment, satisfaction and determination required in modern industry, let alone the high standards of quality, will not be obtained from workers that do not have the slightest chance of owning the products they work their butts off to make every day. That may have been possible in the past, but no more.

Once again, the right corporate strategy will be to get as close to the customer as possible. But that means being close to the average *Brazilian* consumer, who by definition is in an entirely different income bracket from the one uppermost in the minds of most multinational managers.

We must change many things. The starting point is the basic product itself. Many of the sophisticated technological trappings more suited to the developed-country consumer can be stripped away. Forget planned obsolescence, which leads to a stream of new models and ever-increasing sophistication.

Ninety per cent of Brazilians do not yet own many basic products. Sophistication is dispensable in a first purchase. George Bush, former president of the United States, complained that he did not know what all those buttons on a videocassette recorder were for. You can imagine what happens to a Brazilian consumer faced with his or her first VCR.

Instead of encouraging the return of the Volkswagen Beetle, the Brazilian government should have hyped bicycles as the solution to our transportation problems. The VW Beetle costs between US$7,000 and US$8,000. Few Brazilians can pay this price. A bicycle, on the other hand, could cost between US$200 and US$300, an affordable price for people earning average income.

India has solved its transportation problem with the introduction of a motor scooter for three. China is the world's largest manufacturer of bicycles. The Chinese have found out that the bicycle is the most suitable means of transportation for their development stage and for the income level of their population.

Some cities have realized the benefits that bicycles can bring and have started to include them in their urban planning. Ribeirão Preto, in the state of São Paulo, has brought an expert from Australia to plan and build its first street for bicycles only. Changes like this cannot be operated without government participation. Some traffic laws will certainly have to be rewritten.

One of the most important challenges to those who want to enter the low-price product market is cost-effectiveness, or the relationship between price and quality. It is of fundamental importance to fine-tune this duo in order to ensure that higher-quality products are not unaffordable for Brazilian consumers.

Packaging is certainly one of the most important items that contribute to the price of a product. In 1994 Batavo, a dairy foods firm in Paraná, launched a yogurt in family-size packaging. A one-liter plastic bag replaced five 200-gram pots, the traditional packaging. The price dropped 50% thanks to the savings obtained solely through new packaging – and it was a resounding success. Competitors immediately followed suit, since the new packaging does not affect product quality.

In New York you would not dream of building a large shopping area without direct access by subway.

Companies will also have to rethink the question of distribution channels. In fact this is one area that will undergo an enormous revolution in Brazil. Marble-paved shopping malls will certainly place products out of reach of the average consumer.

Low-income consumers not only lack money to buy more; they also lack time. That is why it is hard to understand why no space has been provided for retailers near subway stations in big cities like São Paulo. Few stores are to be seen next to or above subway stations in Brazil.

In New York you would not dream of building a large shopping area without direct access to a mass transportation system. The city's most famous and sought-after stores, Macy's and Bloomingdale's, are located next to subway stations.

It is imperative to evolve from the traditional system of sales through stores. Access must be given to more consumers through such new channels as telemarketing, mail order (which will boom now that catalogs with fixed prices are possible because of low inflation), and factory outlets, which bring down distribution costs, to mention a few.

Statistics show that by the year 2000 three-quarters of the population will be in the low-income bracket.

When we have developed the capability of producing cheaply and in large quantities, we will be able to export much more to the third world to China, India, Greece, whose demographics are similar to Brazil's.

We must think on our feet so that we can revolutionize corporate strategy and stop producing articles full of bells and whistles for the developed world, in order to explore the potential of exporting to low-income countries with similar consumption patterns to our own. Statistics show that by the year 2000 three-quarters of the world population will be in the low-income bracket.

This also leads to a change in advertising. Models who portray middle-class ethnic features and consumption habits will not be suitable for the new markets.

A good current example is a TV commercial for 'Antarctica' beer. It shows an informal group playing samba, with a majority of blacks, rather than a lone token black to demonstrate political correctness. The commercial was certainly not inspired by any ideological principle, however, simply by good business principles. The new development cycle, which in fact started in 1992, should last until the year 2005. The main reason for predicting a limit to this growth period is that it is not yet possible to quantify Brazil's ability to take on China and India, our biggest competitors in the year 2000.

If Brazil is capable of making a qualitative leap in these ten years, it will have climbed a few rungs higher on the ladder of per capita income and will be producing different products, thus no longer competing with the Chinese on the same level. If we miss the boat and keep marking time, year after year, owing to monetary instability and a stop-go economy, we will reach the year 2005 competing eyeball to eyeball with countries like China and India.

Denationalization of the economy is one of the prices we must pay for ten years of bad economic management.

No-one is arguing that all our problems are over. My contention is that our problems will be of a different nature: they will be growth-related rather than inflation-related. We will face difficulties in this new decade of development, but many of them will be new ones.

The first difficulty, ironically, will be management of this growth. We are not prepared for it. Businessmen are slowly realizing the possibilities. Before so patiently reading this book, my faithful reader probably had no idea that things in Brazil are so much better than conventional wisdom dictated, let alone that the local subsidiary is preparing for accelerated growth.

New funding rules will come with this new cycle of development. They will exclude privately-held corporations. Businessmen who insist on keeping control totally within the family will probably find they do not have the resources to grow their business. Reinvested earnings will not be sufficient for the new growth cycle, although they were in the past. Profit margins will be much lower this time around, and industry is much more capital-intensive.

Companies' biggest problem in the new growth cycle will be how to retain their most competent personnel.

The great challenge will be in human resources. During the recession of the nineties, brought about by the economic policies of Mr Collor and his intellectual mentors, most companies threw out their corporate training programs in order to save cash. So it will not be surprising to see most companies filling new staffing requirements with employees successfully raided from competitors. Where else can they get qualified people?

The last thing your company wants during a rapid growth period is a competitor raiding your staff. How will firms retain their best employees and managers? Management problems and technical questions can be solved either by hiring consultants or by bringing in technology. But no company can overcome the loss of its most qualified personnel.

There will be a brutal turnover of the most highly skilled executives and personnel in the next few years. Turnover is already high in Brazil, and a three-year recession leaves a lot of hurt feelings. Many employees are itching to leave as soon as better jobs become available again.

Turnover is already a serious issue: on average, 28% of a company's employees change jobs in a single year. Statistically, at that rate a company will have turned over its entire workforce in five years. This is an obstacle to quality and training programs. With economic growth, thousands of executives and employees who are unhappy with their work but hesitated to jump ship because of the recession will take the first opportunity to change jobs or start their own business.

To prevent personnel flight, firms will have to invent new mechanisms for keeping their people. The most expensive way is to increase salaries at each threat of resignation. There are less expensive ways, such as offering shares of stock not necessarily handing out shares, but making it easier to purchase them.

There are four types of company in Brazil: Type I where only the owner has fun; Type II where only the owner's son has fun; Type III where no-one has any fun; and lastly, the modern company, in which everyone has some fun. A good company to work for is one where Monday is not the worst day of the week nor is Friday the best.

In other words, the best place to work is a company that is open to employees' suggestions, where bosses listen to subordinates, and subordinates feel part of the process because some of their ideas are put into practice. A company where employees do not just obey orders but are part of a team.

CONCLUSION

GROWTH RELATED PROBLEMS

Poverty is still the worst of Brazil's problems, and now that inflation is under control it will become the political issue of the nineties. Curiously enough, one of the reasons for our skewed distribution of income is that for a long time wages were adjusted every month by a price index, not an income index.

Thanks to new production methods, prices of food and many other goods have fallen by 30% in real terms over the last ten years. In the USA, that would mean an enormous increase in purchasing power: someone earning US$1,000 would be able to buy the same goods for US$700 and still have another US$300 to spend.

Not if you were living in Brazil. Over the year your pay would be eroded by inflation to say US$500, but thanks to an indexation clause it would be jacked back up to US$700. Since your wage is pegged to a price index, those price reductions are included and your income is reduced. You get no benefit from cost cutting or learning curves; nor do producers.

Indexation is a God-given protection against inflation, but it also stops people benefiting from productivity and income-generating price reductions. Part of Brazil's poverty is due to the use of the wrong index to protect pay.

The war on poverty is beginning on the right track: curbing inflation. The second step is increasing the productivity of government. One of Brazil's bestselling books, 'Reinventing Government', published by the Ministry of Public Administration, is rapidly spreading the word on government efficiency and how to attain it.

Brazil's problems are not over. The main argument of this book is that the problems of the past that halted growth are gone, and that now we have to deal with growth and backlogs. For those who love problems, we still have plenty, but they are growth-related.

There will be power shortages, a big boom for energy conservation consultants, and expansion for the energy market. Thermoelectricity, with which we are not highly familiar as a water-rich country, will prosper.

The mindset of management, and especially of head offices in New York and Tokyo, is far from being growth-oriented, so local firms will have a competitive advantage from scratch. Most of my foreign clients are still at the analysis stage, wondering whether I just might be right. My local clients are already taking action, and fast.

Most companies pay for detailed Nielsen market share studies, because the only strategy in town used to be stealing your competitors' customers. From now on, however, the strategy will be grabbing the new consumers coming on to the market. Companies are discovering that no-one really knows how big the potential market is, or how fast it is really growing.

Downsizing, downgrading, downtrading were the buzz words of the day until recently. Eliminating layers of management, firing tons of people, discontinuing unprofitable product lines, making it simple those were the main types of action.

Growth is movement in the opposite direction. It means hiring not firing. It means new product lines, innovation, making mistakes. It means chaos and confusion instead of streamlining operations. It also means exciting times, if you are in the lead. Trying to catch up in a growing economy is a drag.

The key to improving performance is to stop trying to foresee the future and start acting making one's own future rather than waiting for it to happen.

For a long time, the strategy preferred by Brazilian companies was to make money by predicting future trends in the economy. The secret of this strategy consisted of hiring economic advisors, preferably professionals who had access to inside information from the economic team in charge of the national economy.

The next step was to adopt measures that yielded high profits resulting from being able to foresee the forthcoming economic plan. These profits were short-lived, however. Companies became dedicated to speculation and arbitrage, turning their backs on market challenges. Without realizing, they encouraged speculation instead of entrepreneurship.

The slow decline of the role of the economist who looks into his crystal ball is due in large part to redemocratization of the political system and, by extension, the economy. The strategy now, as the economy is irreversible opened up, is to acquire the ability to adapt swiftly to the new reality, in Brazil and worldwide.

The media started to reflect this trend clearly in the mid-eighties, when more prominence was given to news of the business world. Business news started taking up some of the space formerly reserved for heralding economic decisions made in Brasília. And the inevitable conclusion is this: if we cannot depend on ⁺he government, let us depend on ourselves.

There were many years of unsuccessful economic experiments. Executives and employees, treated like guinea pigs, had little influence on the future of their business or the management of the national economy. It was a time of low self-esteem, depression, and lack of motivation.

One of the markets that will undergo tremendous initial growth in the next few years is what I call the market for 'small luxuries'. Brazilians will start to reward themselves again with little treats, after ten years virtually without self-indulgence. There was no spare cash for celebrations in the eighties for eating out, travel, fancy clothes etc.

Fortunately, we have emerged from this stage of our collective lives. We have slowly recovered our ability to influence political and economic decisions, and nowadays there is no more room for government economic plans that usually destroy the best corporate plans.

Executives, entrepreneurs and employees now see their efforts rewarded. Nothing stimulates growth better than success and a feeling of satisfaction at the end of a productive day. Nothing discourages more than stagnation, losses, and dreams left on hold.

Brazil's 1994 GDP is close to the U.S.'s GDP in 1920. Last year Brazil's top 500 firms sold close to what the U.S.'s top 500 sold in 1915. In 1910 the U.S. had 150 million inhabitants, close to our present population of 154 million. In 1910, American firms were discussing how to transform a family-owned business into a professionally managed organization. This discussion is taking place today in Brazil.

In 1890, Mark Twain said that the United States had the best Congress money could buy. In the period 1910-1930, American businessmen were arrogant know-it-alls, as befits self-made men. Today few businesses succeed without a team which shares in the glory and recognition.

Many of Brazil's traits and faults could no doubt be found in the U.S. of the 1920s. For some people, this means we are 70 years behind. Others may argue that Brazil just might be in for a very exciting 70 years with the additional advantage that, like the Great Depression in the U.S., our big recession is already behind us too.

A large part of our future growth will come from making up for time lost during the frustrating eighties. But the economy is already moving forward again. Self-esteem is slowly emerging as the nation retrieves its ability to believe in itself. Far-fetched as this may sound to many Brazilians, the future is starting to take shape. For those who believed that Brazil would forever be the country of the future, I have a piece of bad news. The future has finally arrived.

Figure 27   Brazil's GNP resumes growth.

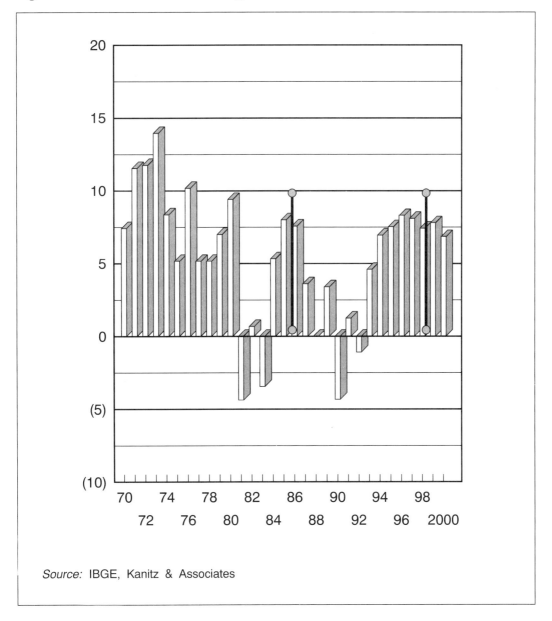

Source: IBGE, Kanitz & Associates

In 1993, Brazil reached the end of a period of poor performance and GNP started growing again. This signaled a new development cycle that will extend until 2005.

Figure 28   GNP growth in 1993 (%).

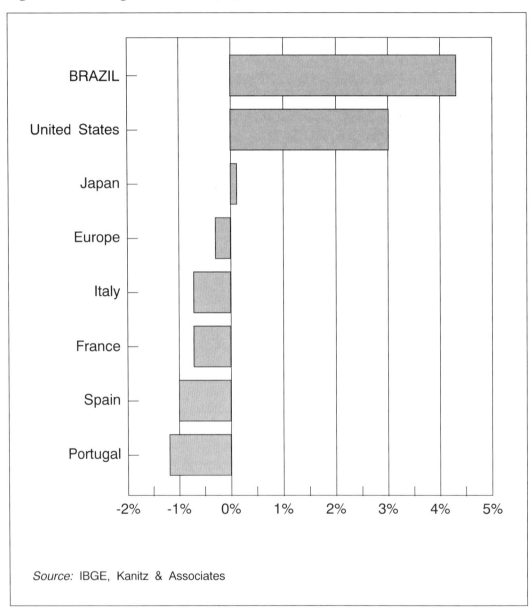

Source: IBGE, Kanitz & Associates

The following three charts, which compare Brazil's GNP in 1993, 1994 (forecast) and 1995 (forecast), clearly point to economic recovery.

Figure 29   GNP growth in 1994 (%).

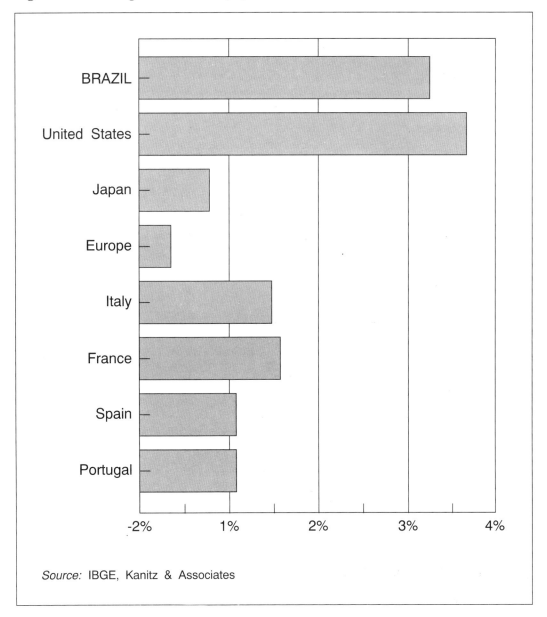

Source: IBGE, Kanitz & Associates

Figure 30   GNP growth in 1995 (%).

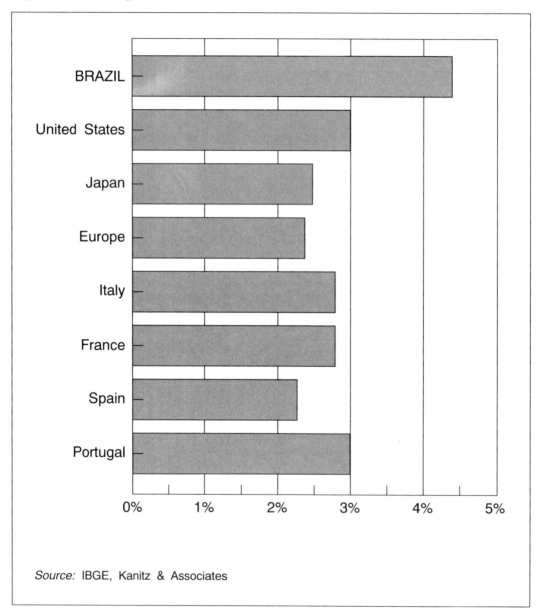

Source: IBGE, Kanitz & Associates

Impressão e acabamento
(com filmes fornecidos):
EDITORA SANTUÁRIO
Fone (0125) 36-2140
APARECIDA - SP